瘋魔杖

圓幻大師口述

明空師兄演像

FOREWORD

Ever since the publication of the "108 Movements of the Shaolin Wooden-Men Hall", a book being rewritten from one among my personal collections, I have received, from time to time, inquires from readers throughout the world, as to what other valuable books I have collected. Some readers (enthusiastic martial-artists, I presume) even went as far as requesting me to sell to them some "valuable" manscripts which I treasure. "I can offer you any price, if the book is a real valuable one...", an enthusiastic reader wrote to me.

The question does not lie in what price some one is willing to offer, nor whether it is a manuscript or the "only copy" as it is called, still less whether this book is an ancient one or a newly published one.

To me, a martial-art book, if it is to be regarded as "valuable", is one that allows the reader to obtain valuable unique martial-art knowledge and understanding. A martial-art book that presents usual unattractive descriptions, or a so-called "special book" that contains something being passed from mouth to ear, is one that seems to be of little use to a beginner of the martial-arts, or a reader who has no previous martial arts knowledge. It also is no help to one who has already obtained martial-arts knowledge.

What is even worse, there are some swindlers in the martial-arts circle, who have no martial-art foundation at all. They try to collect a few photographs and put together some broken descriptions which they copied from other martial-art books, add some groundless "opinions" of their own, publish it, and call it a book of "So & So Style", proclaiming themselves as the writer, the title of so and so "master", or experts of the 7th Dan or 8th Dan "Black Sash" or whatever (My God! Chinese martial artists never use their black sashes for degrees!) They are in fact publicizing themselves to earn money with a low-rated book. A martial-art book of this type has no value at all. It does not attract the glimse of a learned reader. But the worst thing is that it misleads a beginner of the martial-arts and future enthusiasts of the arts. It misleads them to think that that is a branch of martial-arts that contains such bad techniques, or to believe the existence of such a messy sect of the martial-arts.

I myself, being one who loves the art of fighting, would not offer to others a copy of a book which I have collected, be it old or new, precious as "the value of several cities" or cheap as a few coins, manuscript or new-priced print one.

This book, the **"Ferocious Enchanted Staff of the Ancient Monks"**, one that I bought for a few Hong Kong dollars (less than the value of one present day U.S. dollar) from a used-books stall by chance when I was a teenager, became one of my treasured collections.

Of the original version of this book, the latter part, the chapter on **"Application"**, contains only descriptions. It has been rearranged by me, and, together with the illustrated "Set of Staff" in addition to some detail directions of movements, was then edited in the English version by Mr. Leung Wai Choy, to whom I also owe my gratitude for the drawings.

I also wish to extend my thanks to Mr. Richard Lee, who rendered the work into English for me.

Leung Ting

Saarbruken,
West Germany,
30th August 1986.

CONTENTS

The Ferocious-Enchanted Staff of the Ancient Monks

Original Author:

Anonym

Rewriter:

Dr. Leung Ting

Drawer:

Leung Wai choy

The Set

Original Demonstrator in pictures:

Monk Ming Hung

Supplier of the Original Information:

Master Monk Yuan Wan

GRIPS

There are two main grips in the staff set. Namely; the "single-hand grip" and the "double-hand grip". Additionally, the double-hand grip can be subdivided into two different forms of holding positions. The **"Yin-sau"** form is to hold the staff with both the palms facing downwards, as in diagram **A**. While the **"Yin & Yang"** form means that one palm is facing upwards and the other is facing downwards, as shown in diagram **B**.

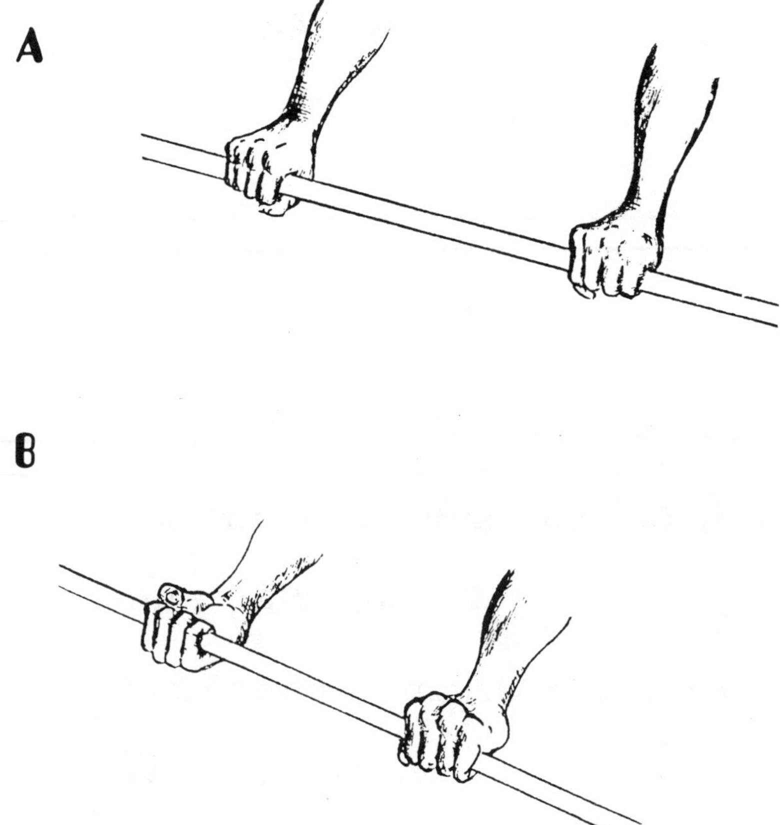

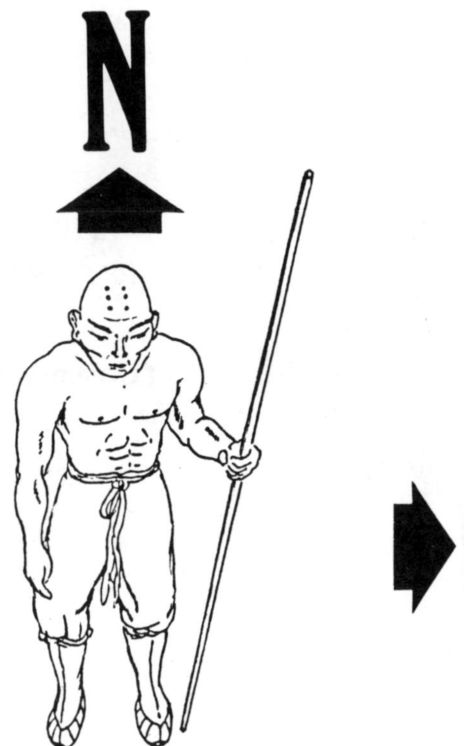

Please pay attention to the positioning of the demonstrator in the following text. We use the four directions as above to fix the exact positions of the demonstrator.

1

(Illustrations 1-5)
"Luminescence of
Buddha's
Aureola"
(Commencement Gesture)

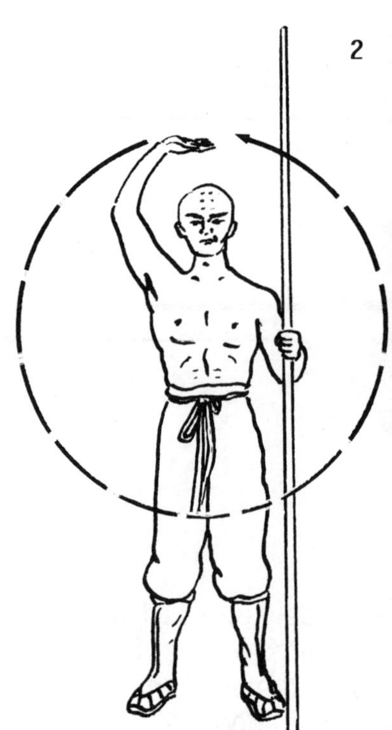

2

3

Left hand holding staff, right hand in front of chest as "worshiper's palm". Right hand is then placed on top of head, it then travels along a large right to left arc before returning to the front of the chest. After that the left foot gives the end end of staff a quick kick causing it to swing up to be caught by the right hand.

4

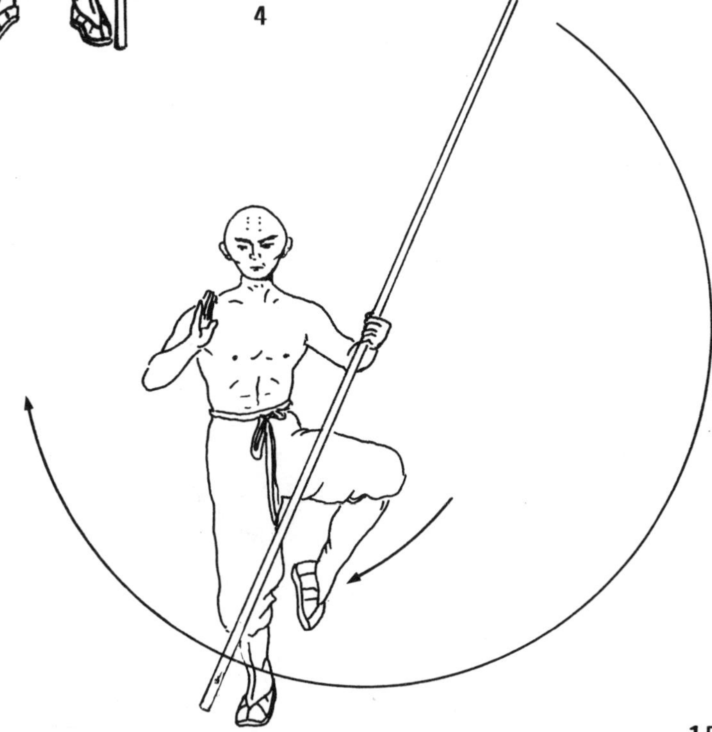

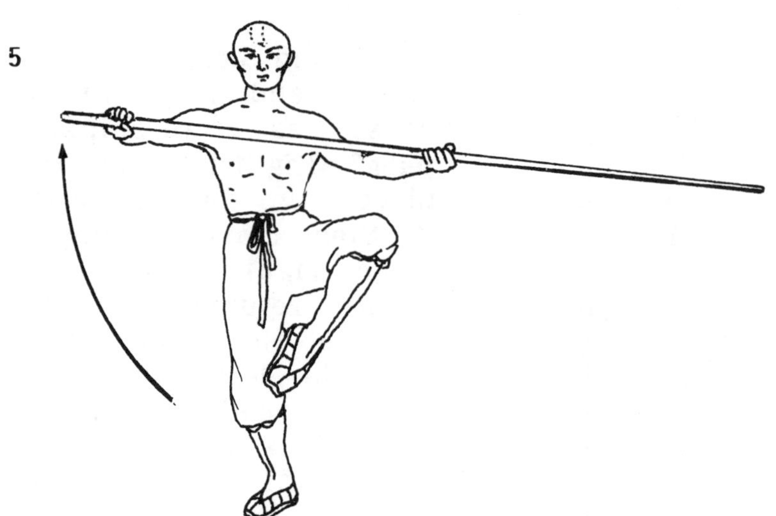

(Illustrations 6-7) "Sweeping Staff"

The staff sweeps from left to right, and then from right to left again.

6

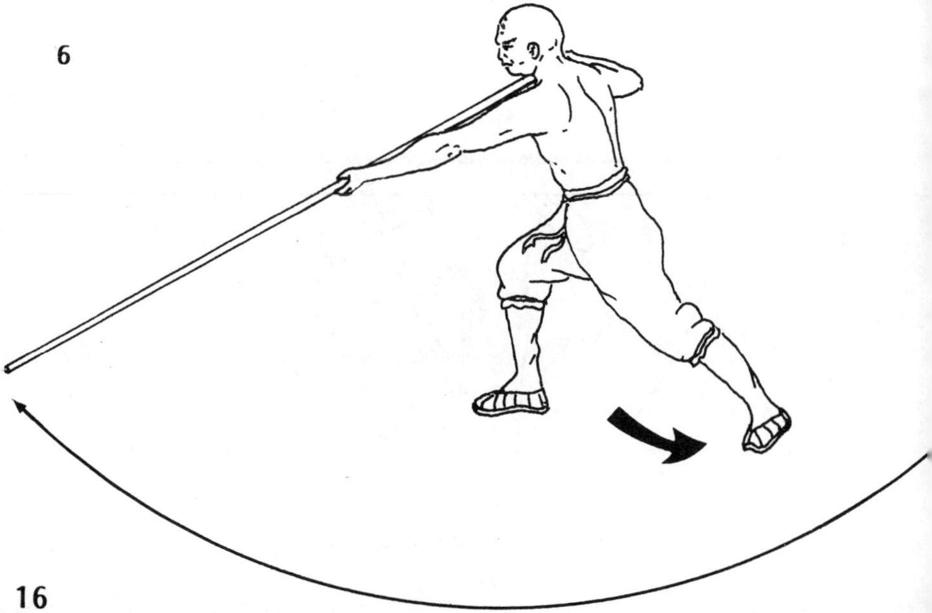

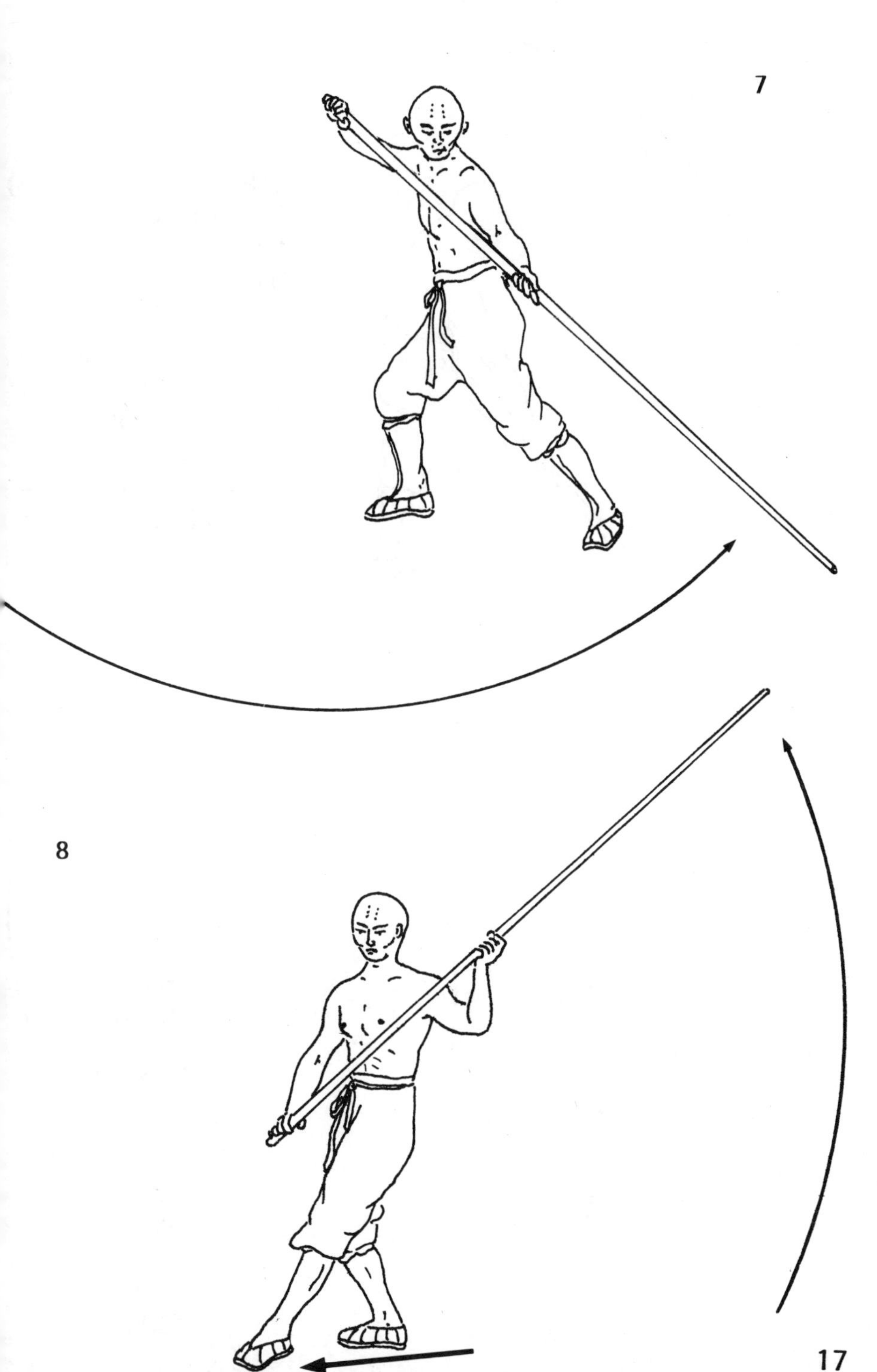
7
8

(Illustrations 8–9) "Downward Chop At Mount Hua"

Right foot makes one forward step. The end of staff is then raised. The staff is made to chop down vigorously.

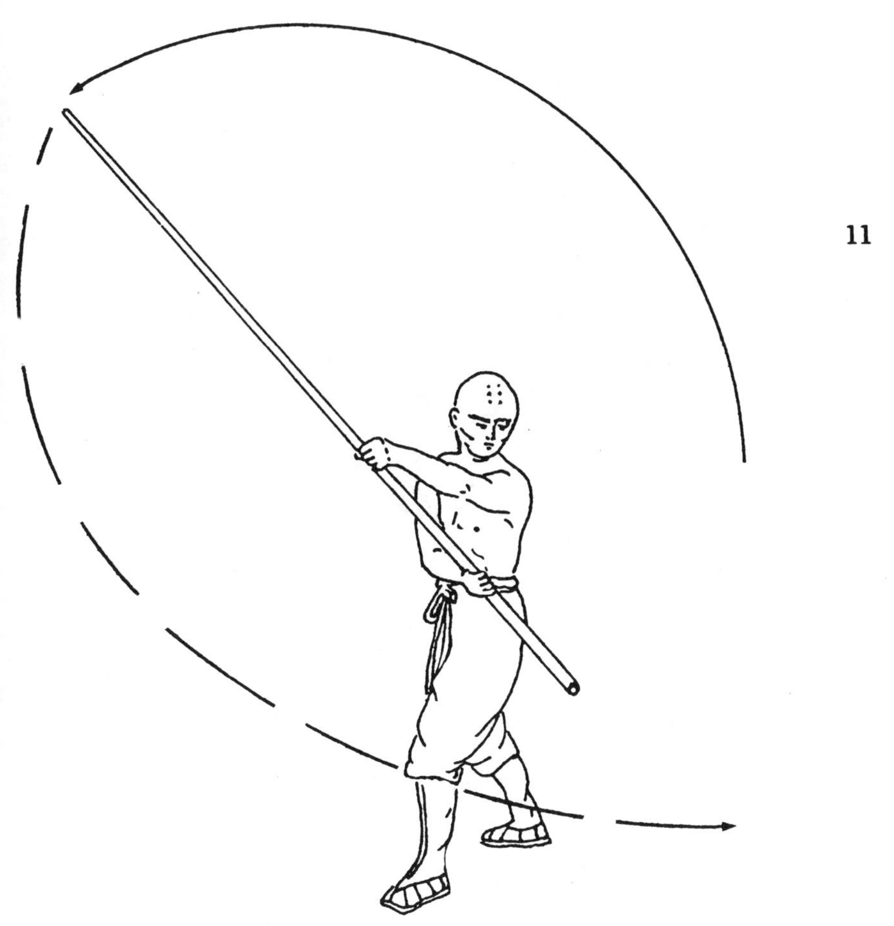

(Illustration 10) "Upward Swinging Staff"

The end of the staff is moved along an upward curved line to execute an upward swinging attack.

(Illustrations 11-12) "The Cracking Whip"

Left hand holding staff. The end of the staff is then swung from the right upper level to the left upper level as the left foot makes a side stride. It makes a cracking sound when done correctly.

12

13

(Illustrations 13-14) "The Whirlwind Sweep"

The left leg leads the body to make a 360° clockwise turn, while at the same time the left hand swings the end of the staff for a circling level turn. If the force is correctly applied, the movement will cause the sound of howling wind and thunder.

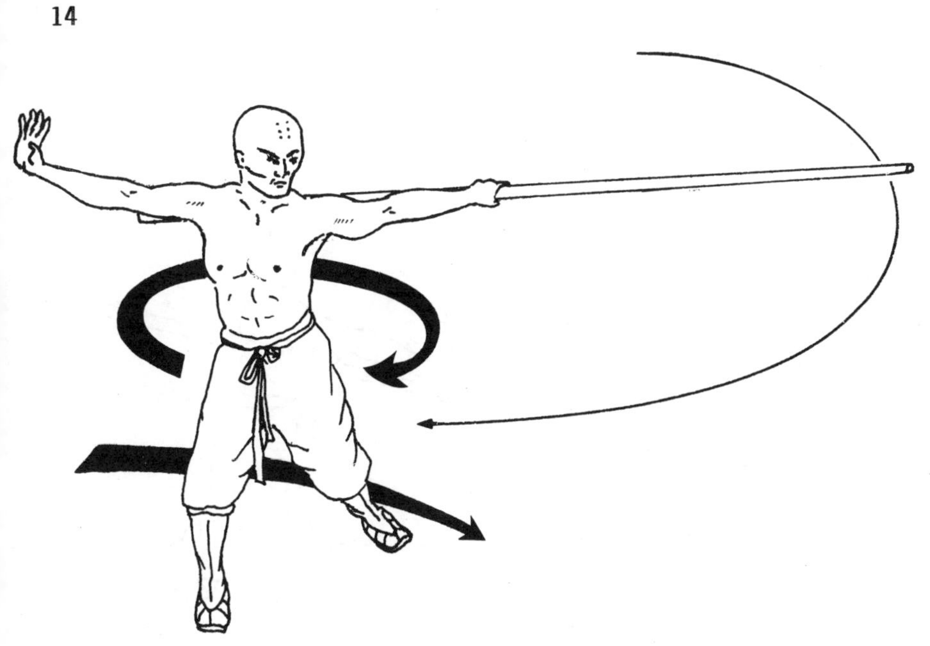
14

15

(Illustrations 15–16) Transitional Movement

The upper end of the staff is held under the left armpit while the lower end is held by the right hand.

16

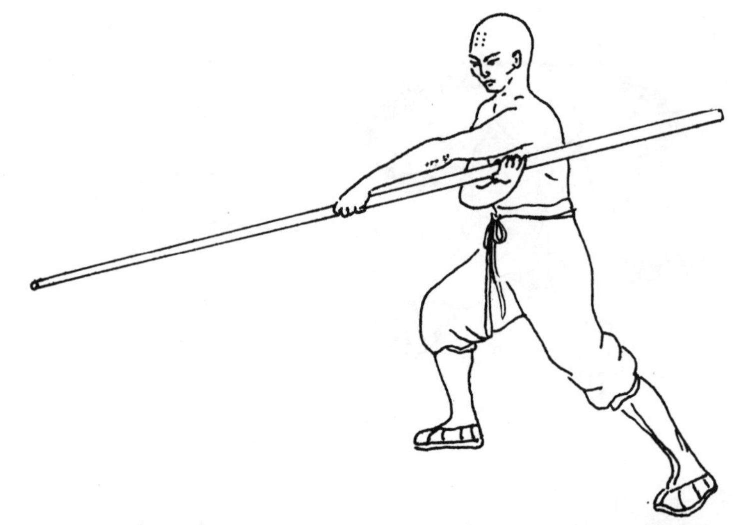

(Illustration 17) "Rise of the Phoenix & Dragon"

The end of the staff is swung upwards swiftly and vigorously so as to cause the sound of wind and thunder.

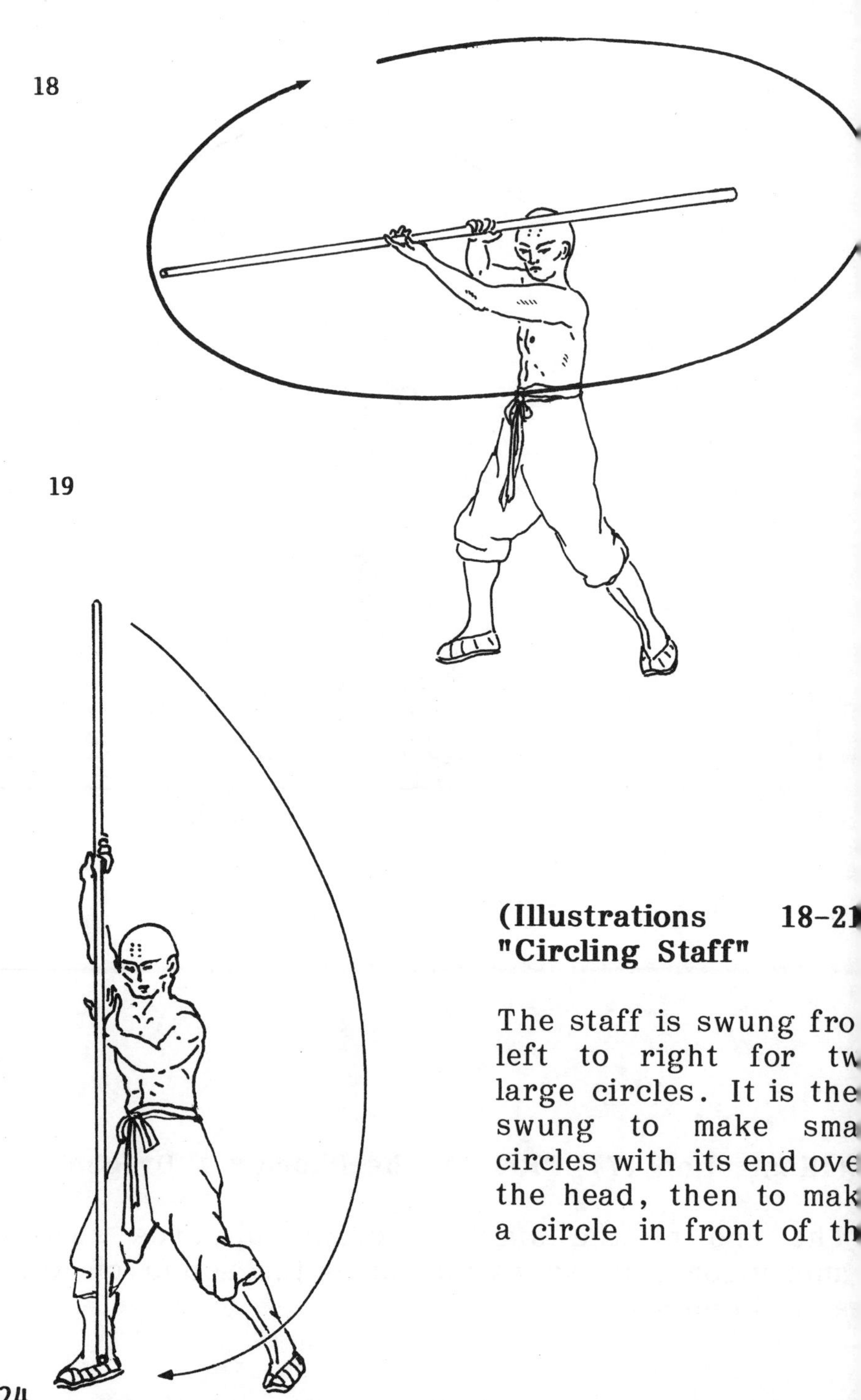

(Illustrations 18–2
"Circling Staff"

The staff is swung fro left to right for tw large circles. It is the swung to make sma circles with its end ove the head, then to mak a circle in front of th

20

body. The last circle is a vertical one made at a low level in front of the body. The staff finally stops and is held with one end pointing up and the other end pointing down.

21

(Illustrations 22-23) "The Sky - high Pillar"

Right foot makes one forward step. The staff is held vertically at the right side of the body.

22

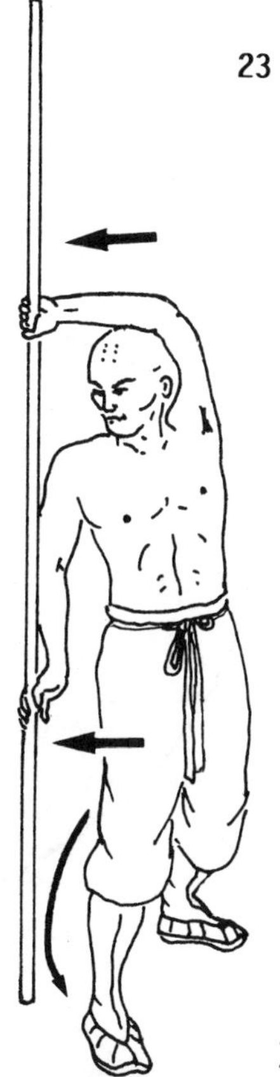

23

24

25

(Illustration 24) "Nod of the Golden Cock"

The upper end of the staff is then swung downwards to make a chopping strike at the right side of the body.

(Illustrations 25-26) "The Thundering Sweep"

The staff is first held by the right hand at the back - the "back holding position". It is then swung vigorously from right to left for a complete circle while the body makes a turn in the same direction. It makes a thundering sound if done correctly.

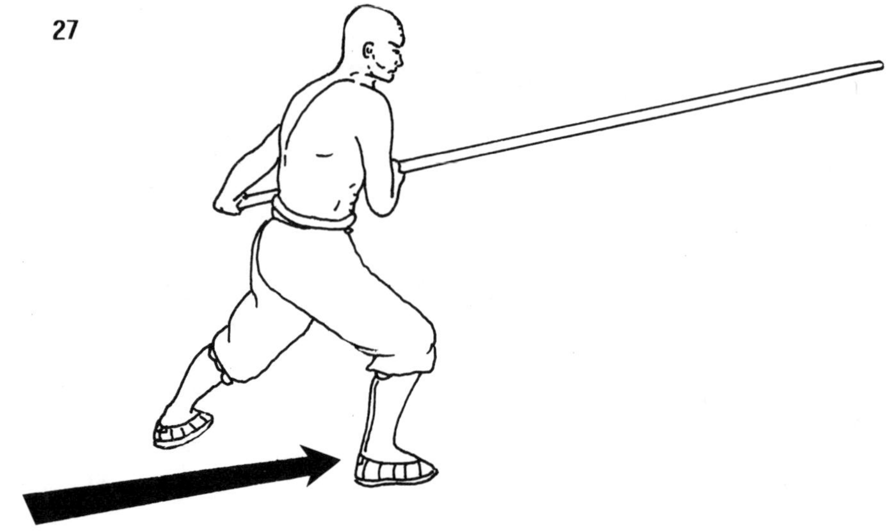

(Illustrations 27-28) "The Throat Dart"

The right foot makes a large forward stride while the end of the staff is thrust forward.

(Illustration 29) Transitional Movement

The staff is then withdrawn, while the right leg poses the hanging stance to get ready for the next movement.

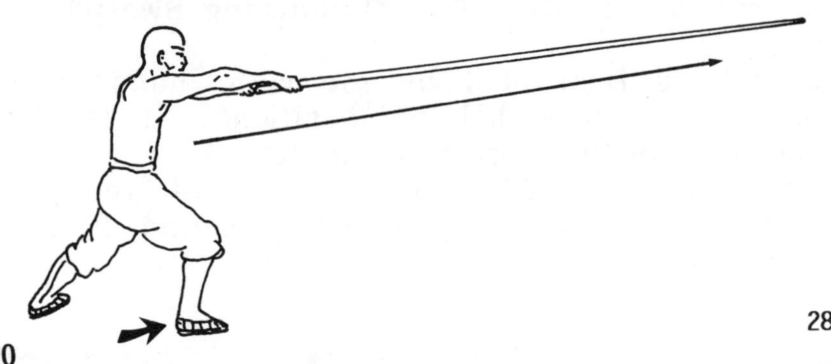

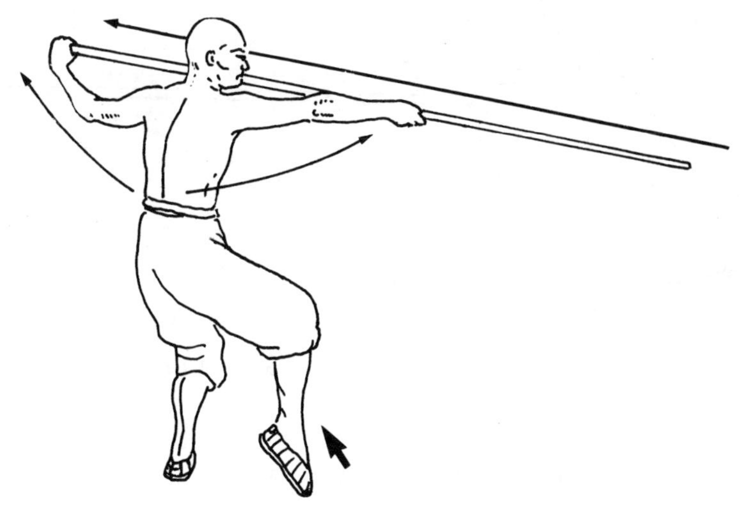

(Illustration 30) "The Tail Sweep"

The right leg makes a left side step thus posing the "Twist Stance", while the end of the staff is swung to the back. It is important that the sight of the eyes follows the travel of the end of the staff.

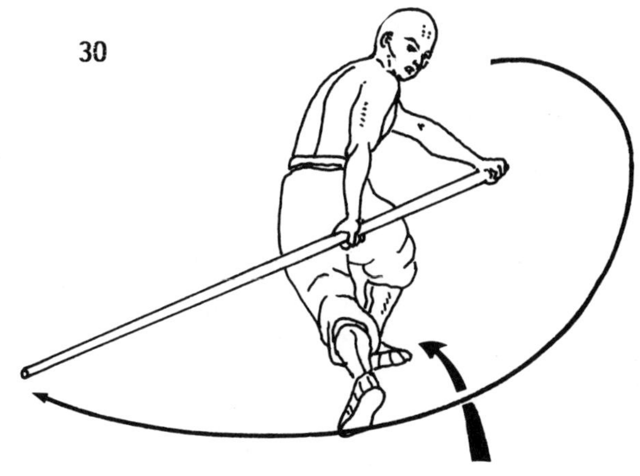

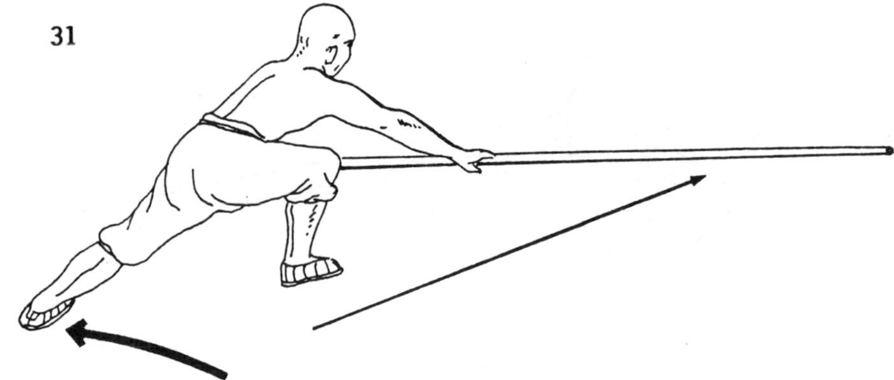

(Illustration 31) "The Cross-Bar Technique"

Using the right foot as the pivot, the left leg leads a left turn while the staff, being held by both hands in the ***"Yin-Sau"*** form *(* the palms facing downwards)*, is swung horizontally at a height of not more than one foot above the ground. This technique is known as "Horse-leg Cutting Staff", and is best applied to deal with a mounted opponent.

(Illustration 32) "The Clearance Sweep"

After applying the Cross-Bar Technique, the body is turned from right to left, at the same time the staff is also being swung to the same direction.

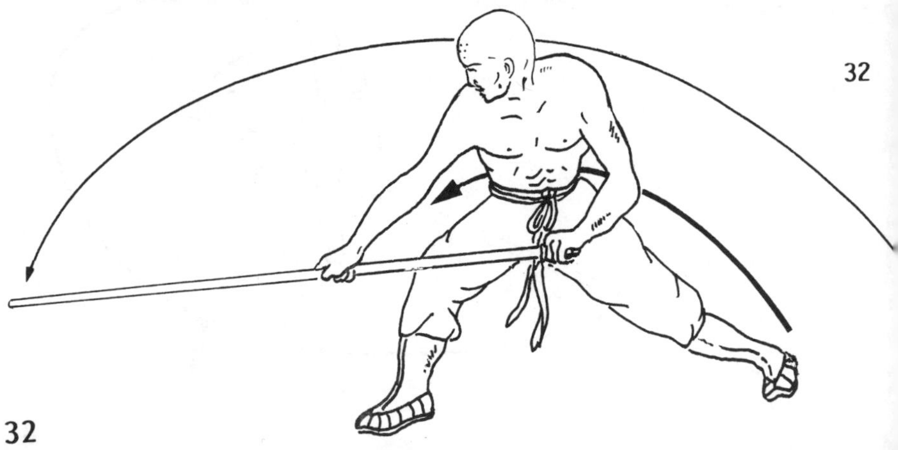

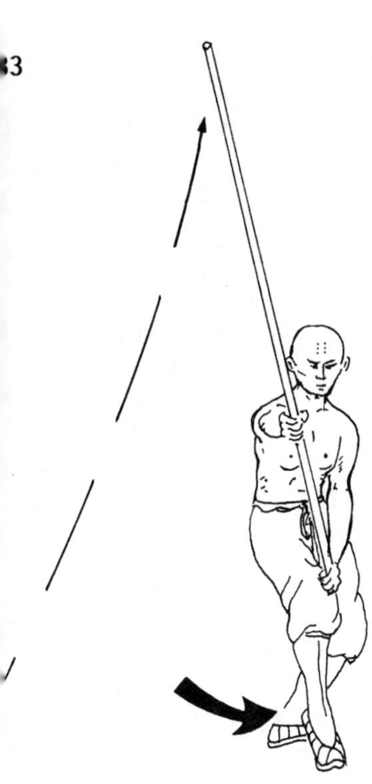

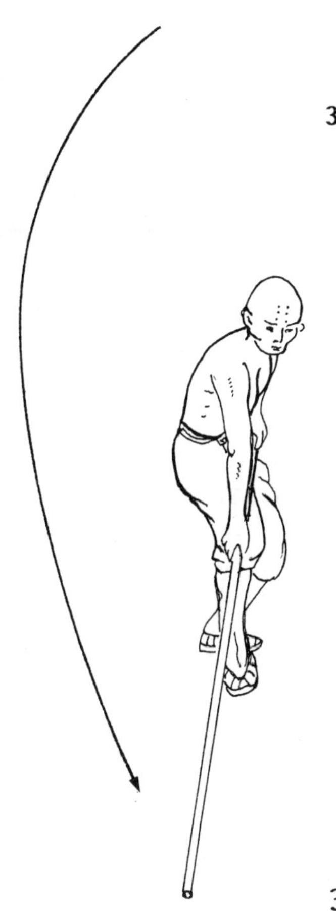

(Illustrations 33–34)
"The Fishing-Rod Technique"

Rise to adopt the right "Hanging Stance". Raise the end of the staff suddenly and vigorously smash it downwards — a movement similar to that of the fishing rod, that is where its name comes from.

(Illustration 35) "Upward Flip On Low Stance"

The right leg is being stretched to the right and rests on the toes of the right foot. The body is lowered, thus forming the "Low Hanging Stance". At this moment, the end of the staff is flipped upwards. If correctly applied, the flip will knock the staff of the opponent out of his hands.

(Illustration 36) "Kneeling On Staff"

Place the right knee on the shaft of the staff, and let the body weight sink onto it. The technique will cause the opponent to drop his staff no matter how strong his arms are.

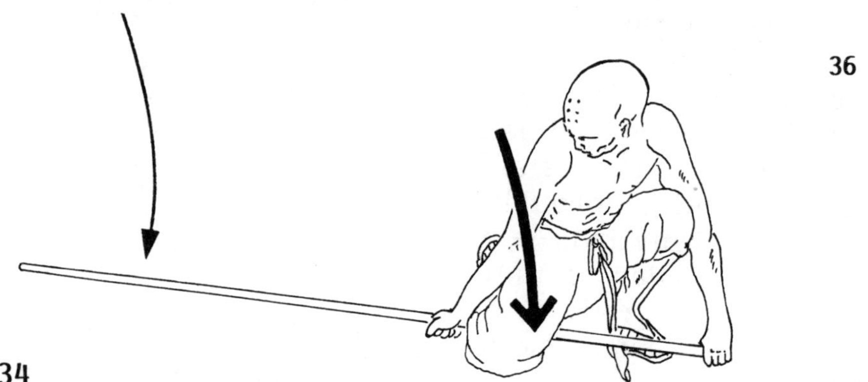

37

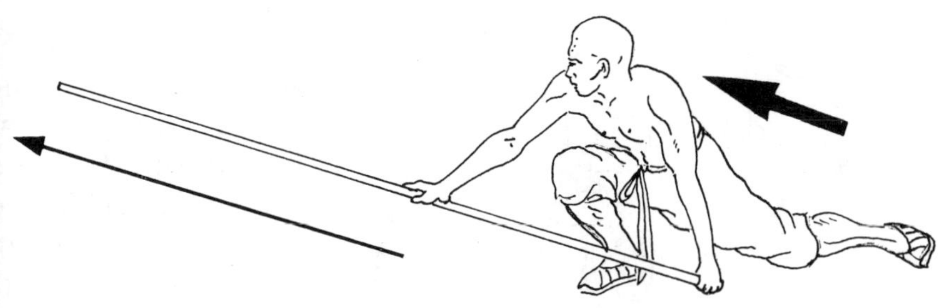

(Illustration 37) "Poisonous Snake Coming Out from Cave"

After that, rise to stand on both feet, and dart the end of the staff straight forwards.

(Illustration 38) "The Backward Swing"

As the tip of the staff reaches the end of its travel, the staff is then swung horizontally from the front to the back, at the same time the eyes follow the travel of the tip of the staff. If correctly Applied, the movement will cause the sound of thunder.

38

39

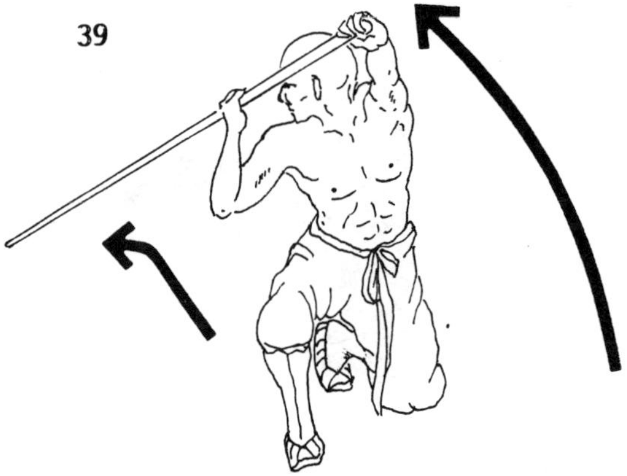

(Illustration 39 "Look Back At th Flower"

Next, point th tip of the staff a the ground, an raise the left han which is holdin the end of the staf to the height of th forehead.

(Illustration 40) "The Rock-Cracking Staff"

The head is then quickly turned to the left front, at the same time the staff, being held at the end with the left hand, is swung downwards from the back. If correctly applied, the movement is so powerful that it will cause the sound of thunder, and a loud crack upon hitting the ground. The staff will bounce up for the next application.

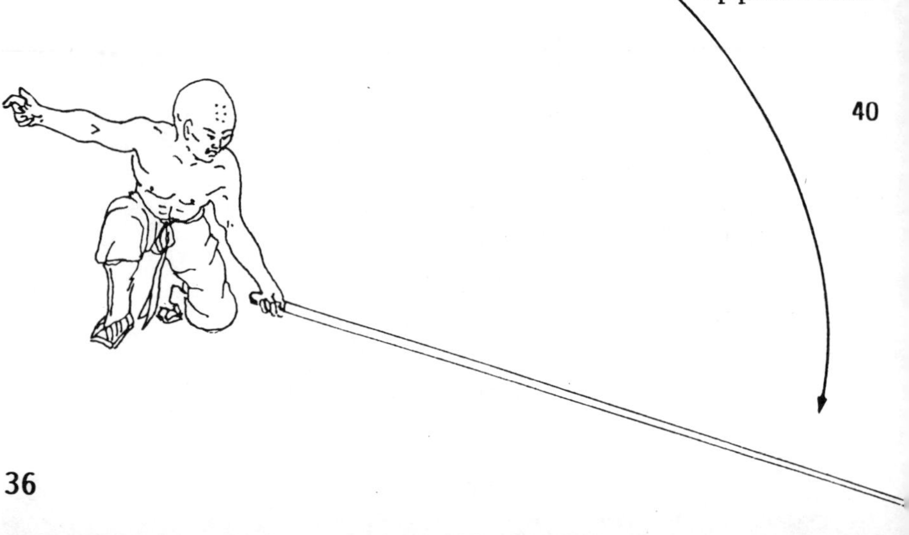

40

41

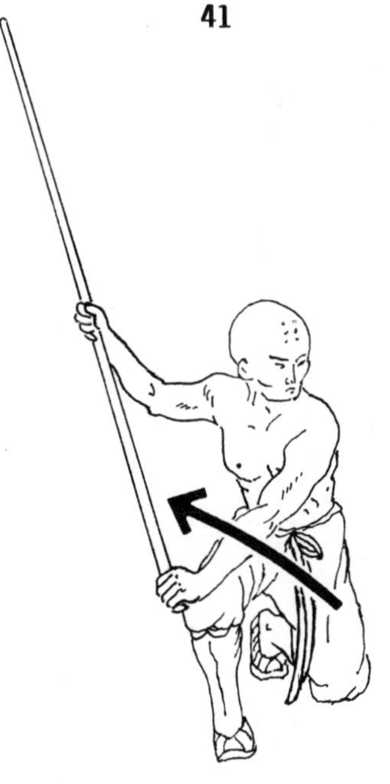

(Illustrations 41–42)
Transitional Movement

On bouncing up, the staff is caught at the shaft by the right hand. The body is then raised to adopt the High Stance.

42

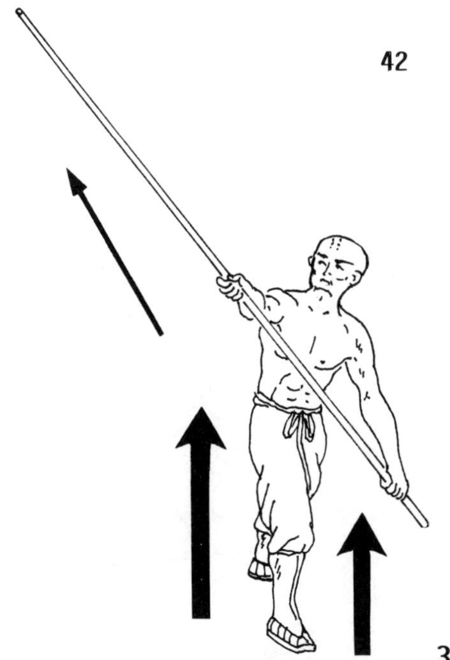

43

(Illustrations 43-44) "The Immortal Pointing The Way"

The left foot makes a forward stride, the staff is raised from the back to the front, until it is levelly pointing to the front.

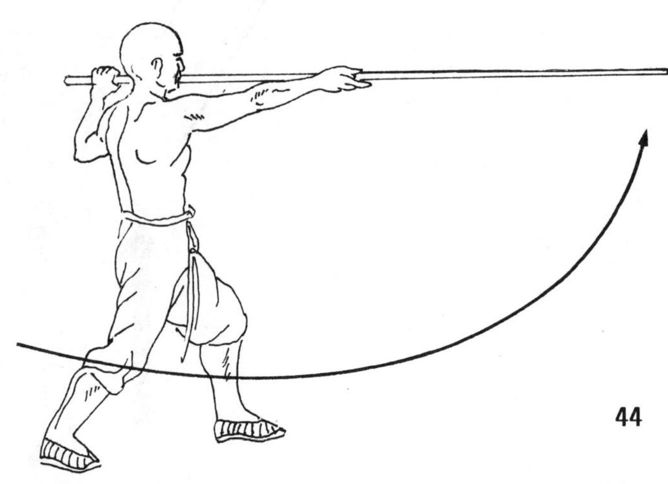

44

45

(Illustrations 45-47) "The Circle Turn"

Using the left foot as the pivot, the body is led to turn for 360°. When turning, the head travels in a level line with the right leg. The movement,

46

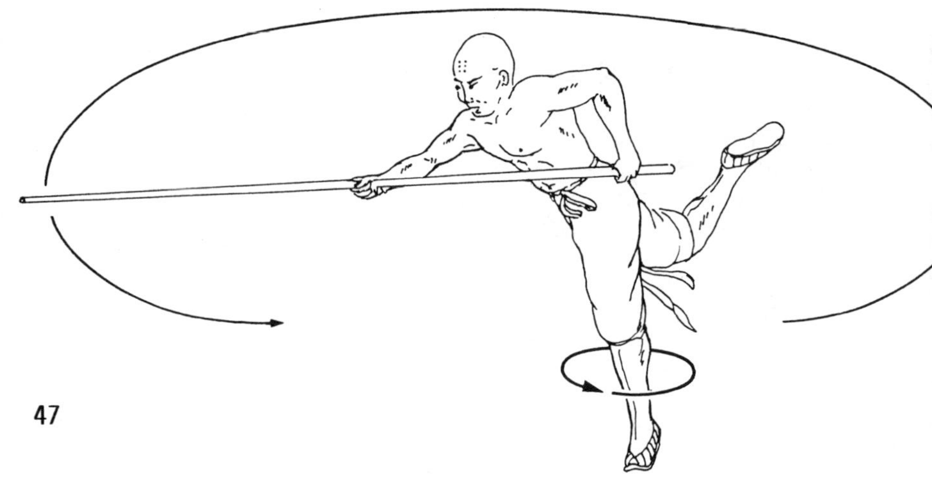

47

though difficult to perform will become easy after ample practice. If effectively applied, it will cause the sound of thunder and whirlwind.

48

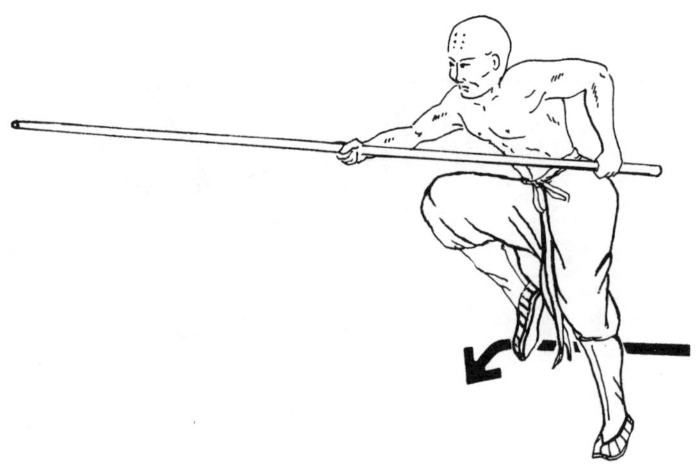

49

(Illustrations 48-50) "The Upward Swing & Slant Thrust"

The right foot makes one forward step. The left hand, while holding the staff, swings its end upwards, until it reaches the height just a little above the head. At this point, the end of the staff is pointing at a forward-downward direction.

50

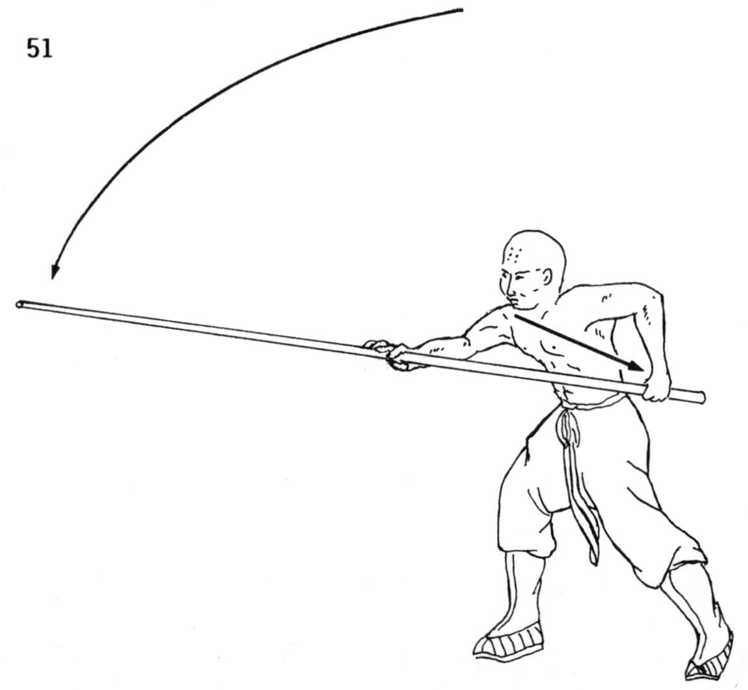

(Illustration 51) "The Downward Smash"

The staff, being held by both hands in "Yin-sau" form, is smashed down from the right upper position.

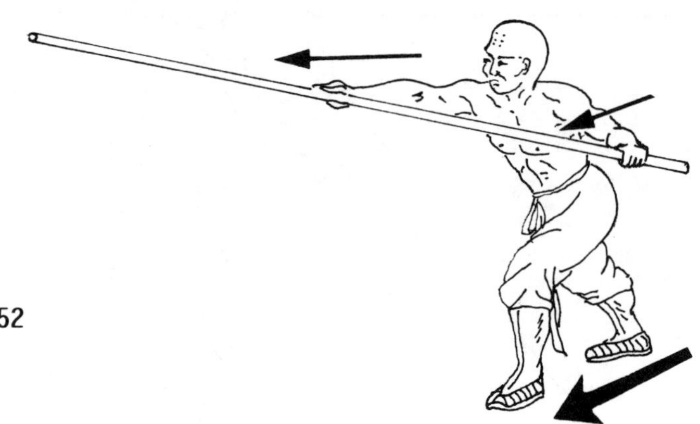

(Illustration 52) "The Horizontal Push"

After that, the right foot makes one forward stride, at the same time the staff is pushed horizontally to the front.

(Illustration 53-54) "Circle & Dart"

The staff, in "Yang-sau" (palm upwards) form with right hand, is being swung for a circle inwards. Immediately after, the tip of the staff is darted forward.

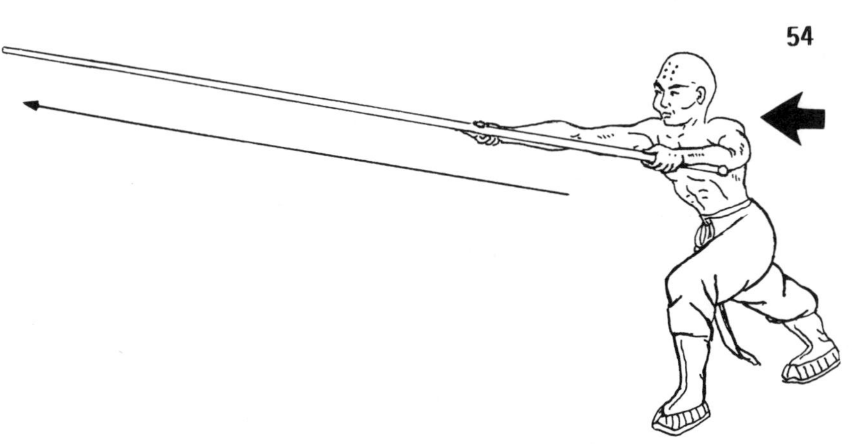

55

(Illustration 55) "The Arhat's Stretch"

The right leg makes one step towards the "north position", as the staff is held horizontally above the head with both arms at full stretch.

56

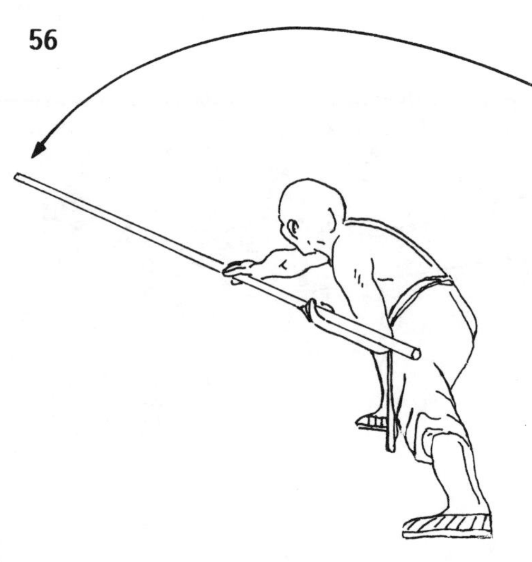

57

(Illustrations 56-57)
"The Slant Smash & Thrust"

The end of the staff is swung down from the right upper position to the left lower position as the body is being lowered to strengthen the smash. Next the body rises to execute a slant forward-downward thrust to the "north position".

(Illustration 58) "The Circling Staff Technique"

First swing the staff for one circle, then turn to face the "west position".

58

59

(Illustrations 59-60)
Chop & Slant"

Raise the staff as high as possible, and then with one loud shout, smash it down vigorously. As the smash is being executed the head should keep looking to the "west position" while the body is being turned towards the "east position" and the left leg is raised to form the "single leg stance".

60

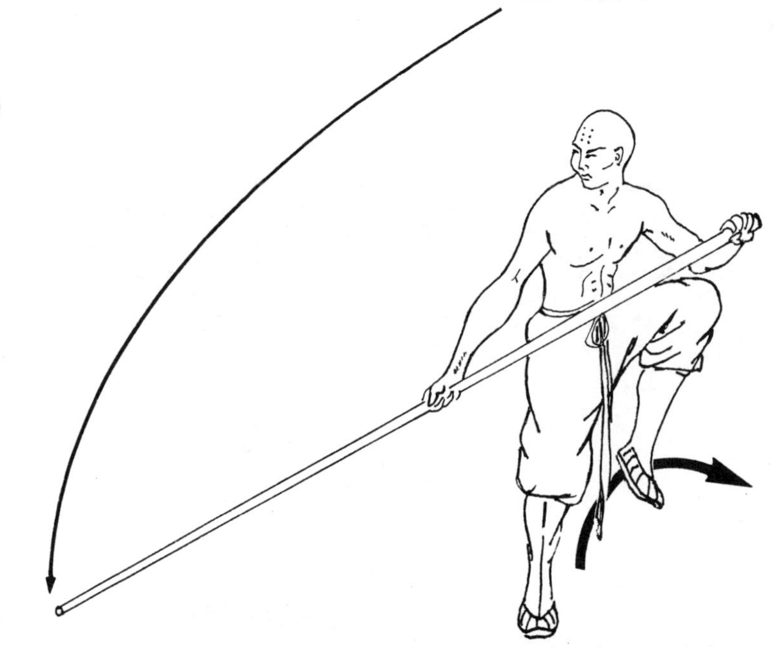

61

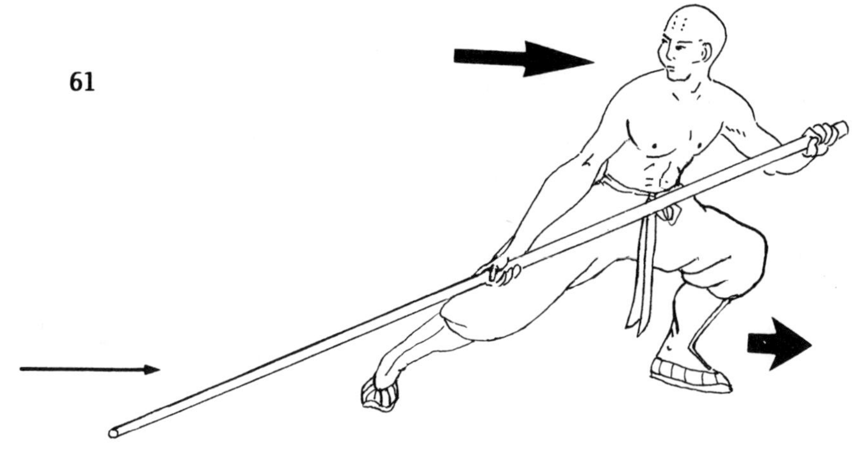

(Illustration 61) "The Dragging Spear"

Point the tip of the staff at the ground while the left leg is making a large stride towards the "east position", and the right leg, being dragged by the left leg, glides over the ground for the same distance towards the same direction.

62

(Illustrations 62-63) "The Backward Dart"

At this moment, the staff is swiftly circled upwards as the body is turned towards the "west position", and then the staff is darted towards the front.

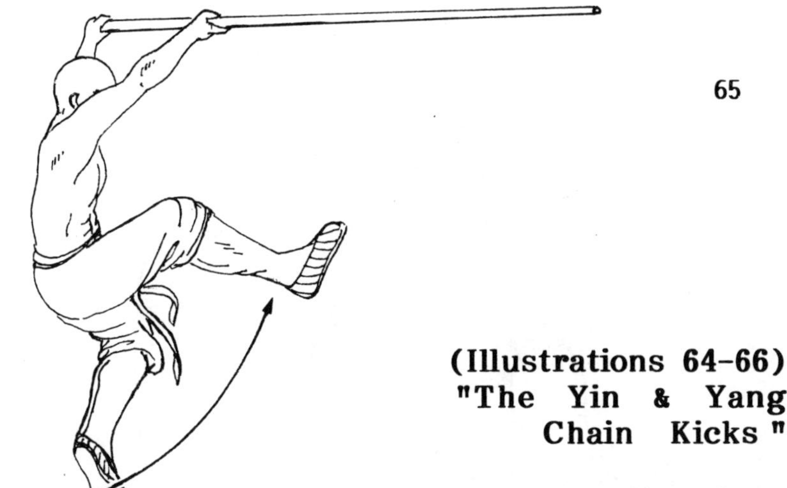

65

(Illustrations 64–66) "The Yin & Yang Chain Kicks "

The staff is first swung vigorously towards the left as the body is turned towards the "east position". When the tip of the staff is pointing to the "east position", the right leg executes a springing kick, and before the right leg is withdrawn the left leg also kicks out. This is what is meant by "Yin and Yang Chain Kicks".

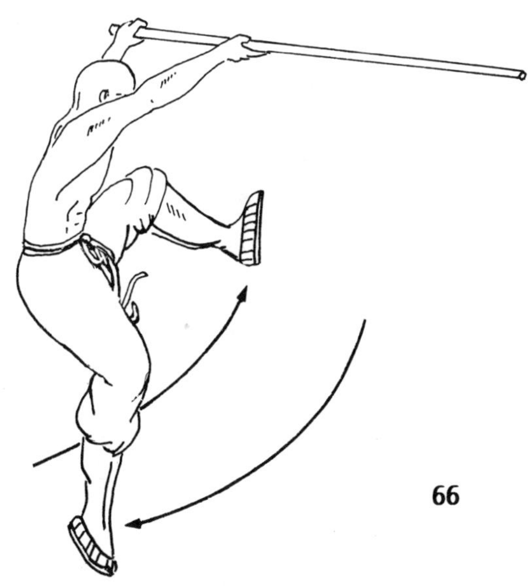

66

67

68

69

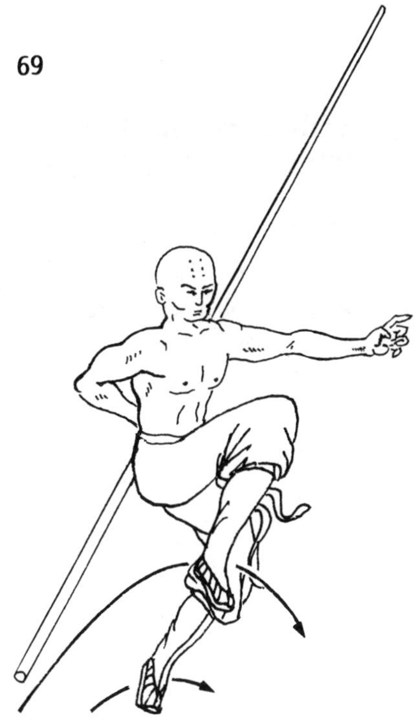

(Illustrations 67-69) "The Monkey King's Leap"

The staff is held at the back with the right hand in the form of "back-holding staff". The left hand is stretched to "claw forward while leaping for a short distance towards the "east position".

70

(Illustration 70)
The Meridian Kick"

While leaping forward the left leg executes kick towards the front.

71

72

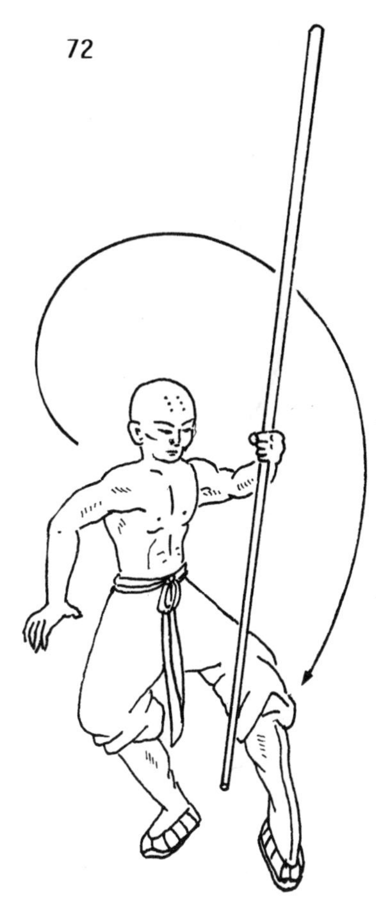

(Illustrations 71-72) "Pull From the Back"

Pose the "Meridian Hanging Stance". Turn the left arm to the back of the left shoulder to get hold of the staff; "pull" it out from behind and place it vertically in front of the body.

73

74
75

(Illustrations 74-76) "Circling Staff Technique"

Swing the staff over the head for two or three circles.

(Illustration 77) "Spinning staff, Single-hand Support"

78

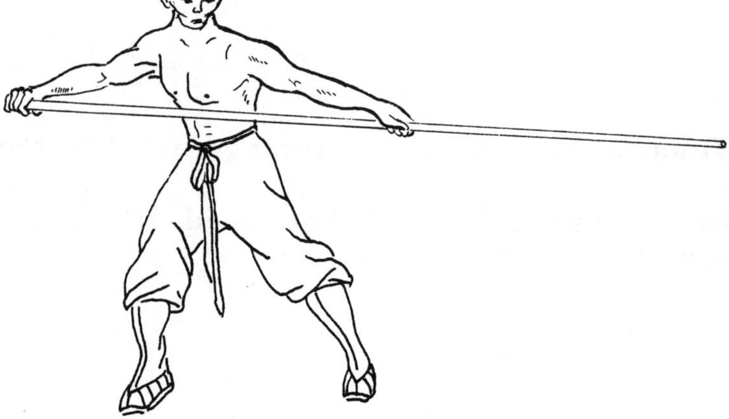

As the staff is spinning over the head, support it at the centre point with the left palm to keep it spinning. To do this with one hand is more difficult than with both hands, and therefore should be practised repeatedly until it can be performed with fluency.

(Illustration 78) Transitional Movement

Next, hold the staff with "yin and yang" hands (one palm-down and the other palm-up holding).

(Illustrations 79-80) "The flying Dragon"

With each hand holding one end of the staff, spin it over the head for one circle in left to right direction. When the circle is completed, spin it in the opposite direction for another circle. The movement will cause the sound of thunder and howling wind.

80

(Illustration 81)
Transitional Movement

Next, hold the staff with the left hand.

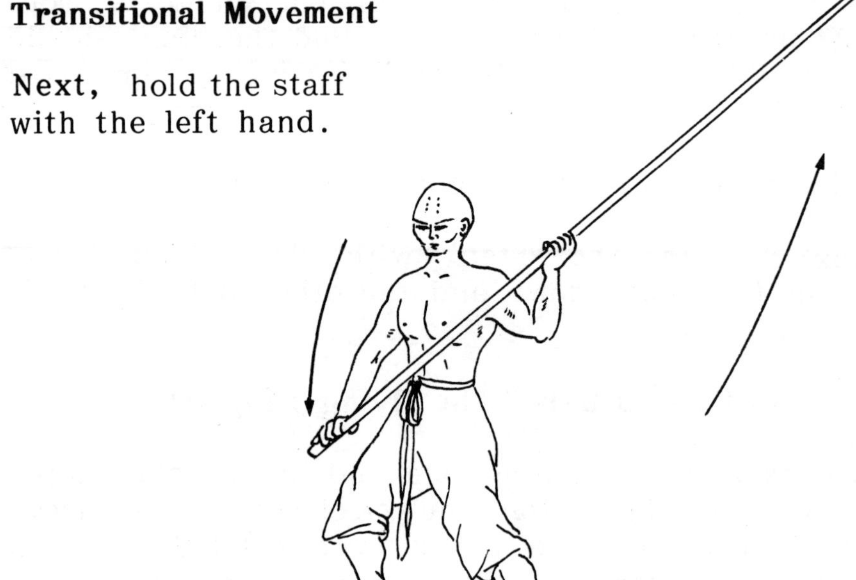

81

82

82

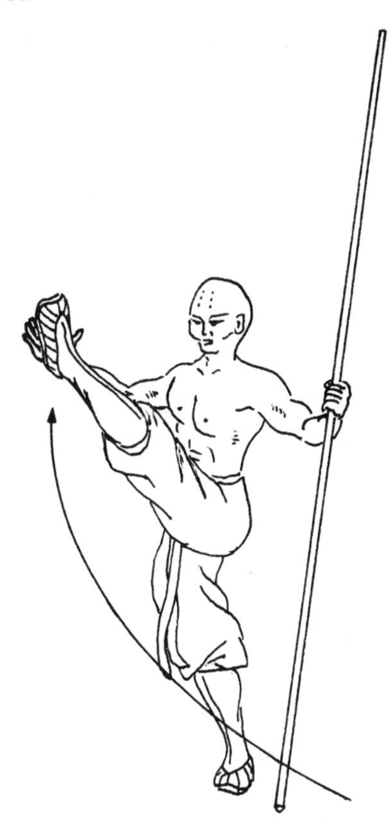

(Illustrations 82-83) "The swallow Tail Kicks"

Hold the staff erect with the left hand. Kick the left leg up towards the upper right position until the instep hits the palm of the stretched right hand, thus making a loud "pop". Immediately after that, the left leg is thrust towards the front. In this technique, two kicks of different directions are being executed one after the other with one leg as if sketching out the shape of the swallow tail, thus getting its name.

83

84

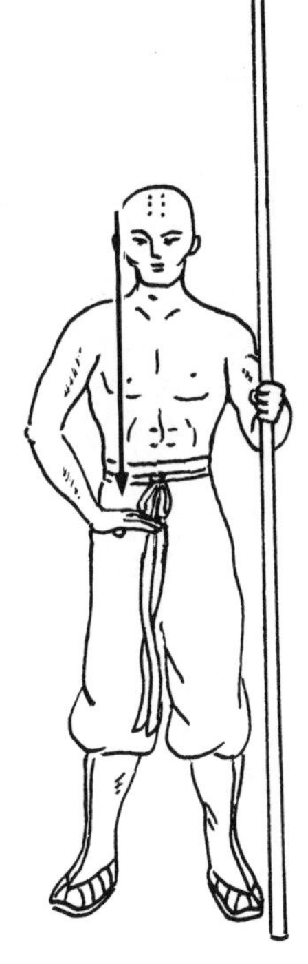

(Illustrations 84–86) "All Powers Submit to the Almighty"

(withdrawal Form)

Stand on both legs. Left hand holding the staff erect at the left side of body. The right palm is turned up and pushed vertically upwards until it is above the head. Then the palm is turned down and thrust swiftly downward-forwards with a deep strong inspiration towards the ***"dan-tien"*** (**to take a breath down deep to the belly —— the translator*). Finally place palms together for a Buddhist salute.

Application

A

B

From "Sweeping Staff" to "Downward Chop At Mount Hua"

The opponent (right) launching "Right Sweeping Staff" at my feet. I counter with the same "Right Sweeping Staff" technique. (If he applies "Left Sweeping Staff", I also counter with the same "Left Sweeping Staff" technique.)

Having blocked his "Sweeping Staff" attack, I immediately apply the "Downward Chop At Mount Hua" technique - a quick downward smash at his head.

From "Upward Swing Staff" to the "Cracking Whip"

If my opponent (left) counters my "Downward Chop At Mount Hua" attack with "The Arhat's Stretch" technique, I swing my staff upwards to get his staff off his hands - a technique known as the "Upward Swinging Staff". Immediately after that, I launch the "Cracking Whip" attack at his flank.

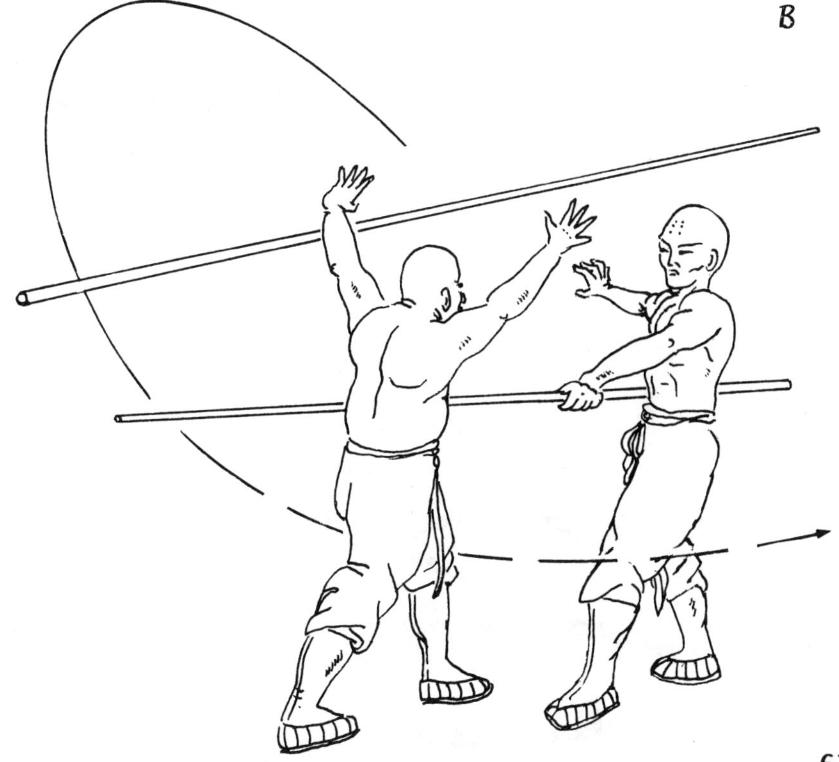
B

"The Cracking Whip" changing to "The Whirlwind Sweep"

The opponent (right) blocks my downward chop attack with the "Sky-High Pillar" technique. I at once change my attack to "The Whirlwind Sweep" technique, thus redirecting an attack at his back.

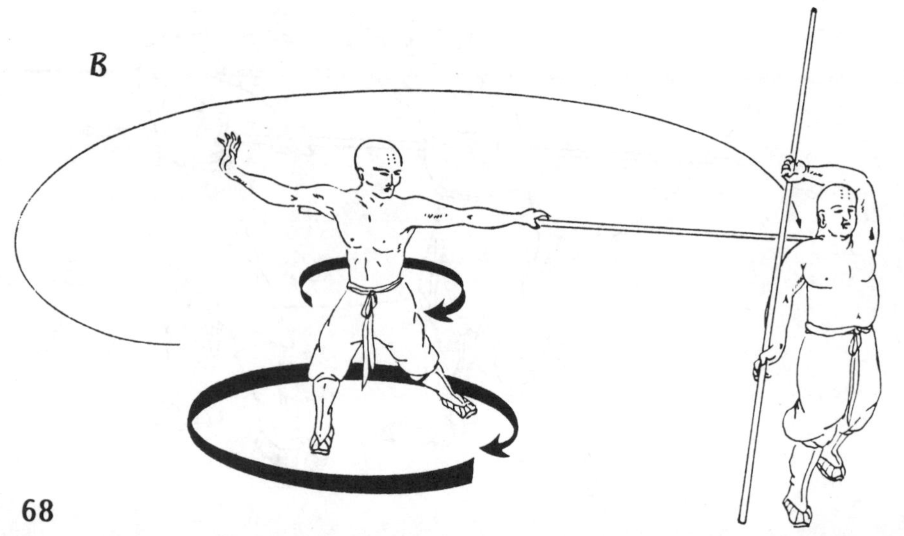

"The Sky-High Pillar" changing to "Nod of the Golden Cock"

Supposing the opponent attacks me with the "Immortal Pointing the Way" technique (illustration 44) or "The Horizontal Push" technique (illustration 52), I can apply "The Sky-High Pillar" movement to block his attack, and then make use of the "Nod of the Golden Cock" movement as a counter attack.

"The Thundering Sweep" & "The Throat Dart"

I face my opponent with the "Staff on Back" posture. If he attacks me with a "Throat Dart", I make a side-step and apply "The Thundering Sweep" technique as defence as well as counter-attack, thus defeating him.

However, if my opponent is aware of my technique, he can step back with "The Immortal Pointing the Way" fashion or "The Horizontal Push" technique to nullify my counter-attack. If that is the case, I shall withdraw my staff and, stepping one pace forward, change it to a "Throat Dart" attack at his throat.

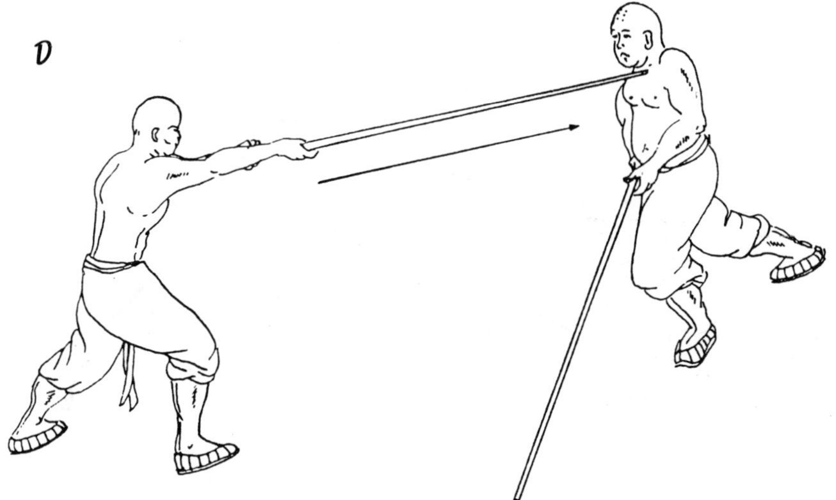

"The Tail Sweep", "The Cross-Bar Technique", "The Clearance Sweep", & "The Fishing-Rod Technique"

Supposing that the opponent attacks me with "The Horizontal Bar Technique" at my lower level, I block his attack with the "Tail Sweep" movement, and, changing it to "The Clearance Sweep", I render a counter-attack at his front. After that, I shall apply The Fishing Rod Technique" - a downward smashing attack at his head.

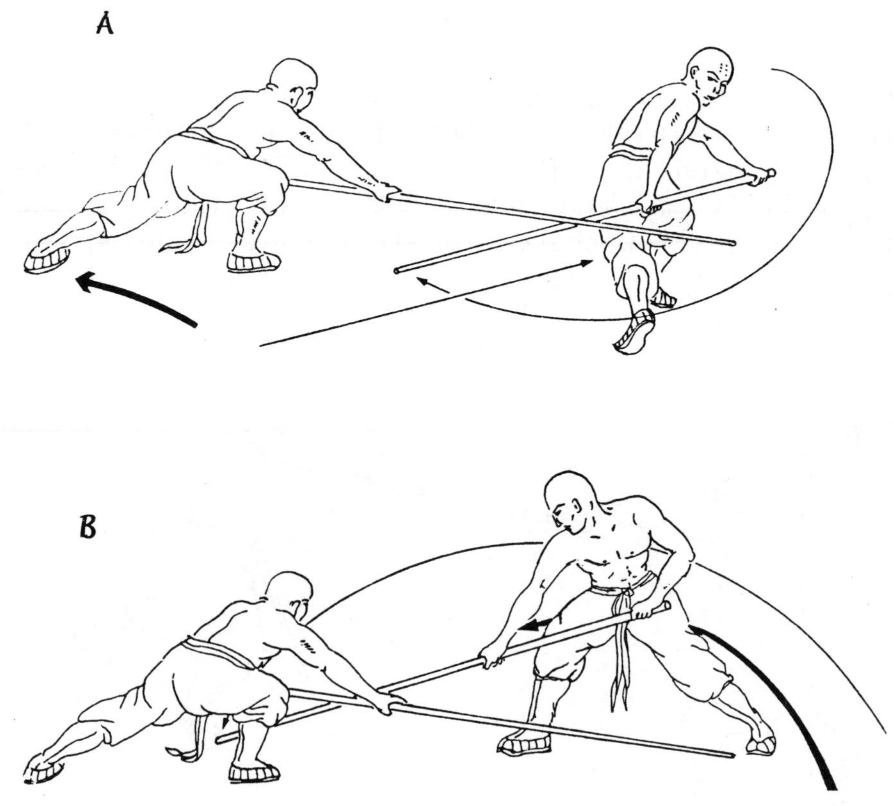

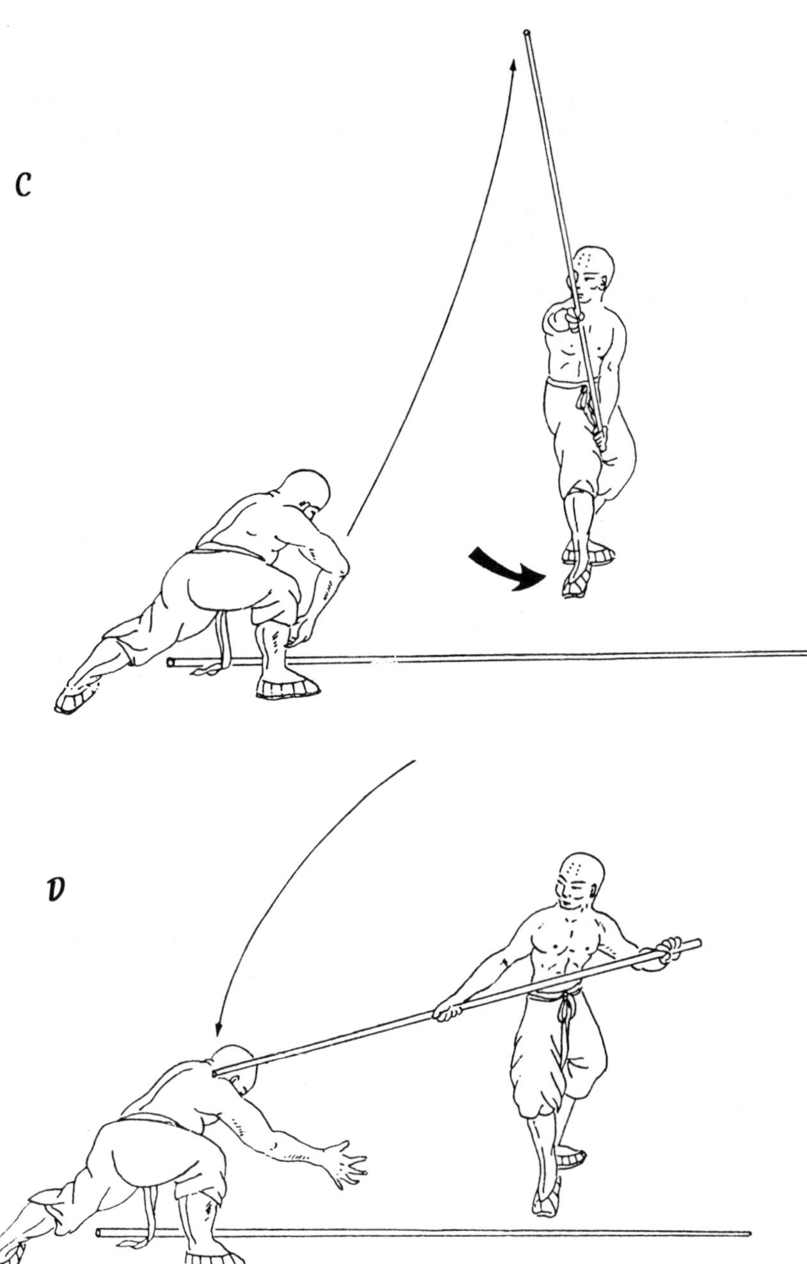
C
D

"Upper Swinging Staff from low stance", "Kneeling on Staff", & "Poisonous Snake Coming Out from Cave"

Opponent attacking me with "Poisonous Snake Coming Out from Cave" technique (left diagram), I block his attack with "Upward Swinging Staff from Low Stance", and changing to the "Kneeling on Staff" technique, I force him to drop his staff. Having disarmed him, I at once change to the "Poisonous Snake Coming Out from Cave" technique, launching a darting attack at his throat.

(My Master's comment: The "Kneeling on Staff" technique is applied in such a way that the whole weight of the practitioner is thrown on his own staff, which in turn transmits the momentous force onto the opponent's staff, thus forcing him to abandon it. This attacking technique can only be nullified at its start with the technique known as "Look Back at the Flower")

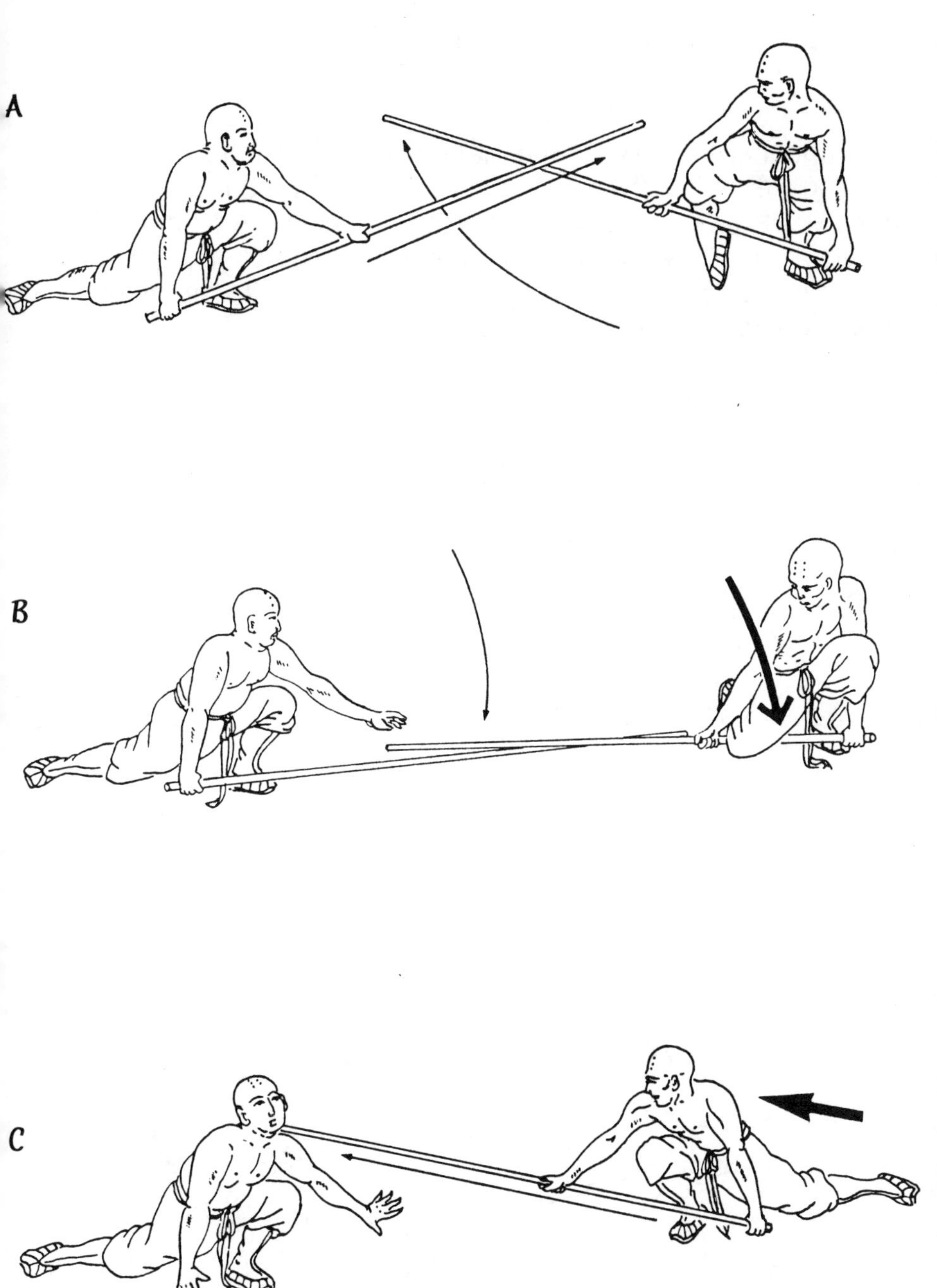
A
B
C

Low Stance "Poisonous Snake Coming Out from Cave" versus Upper Level "Throat Dart"

The opponent (left) and me (right) both holding staff facing each other. Suddenly he launches a "Thoat Dart" attack at me. At this moment, I can first adopt the Low Kneeling Stance, and then apply the "Poisonous Snake Coming Out from Cave" technique to attack his navel part..

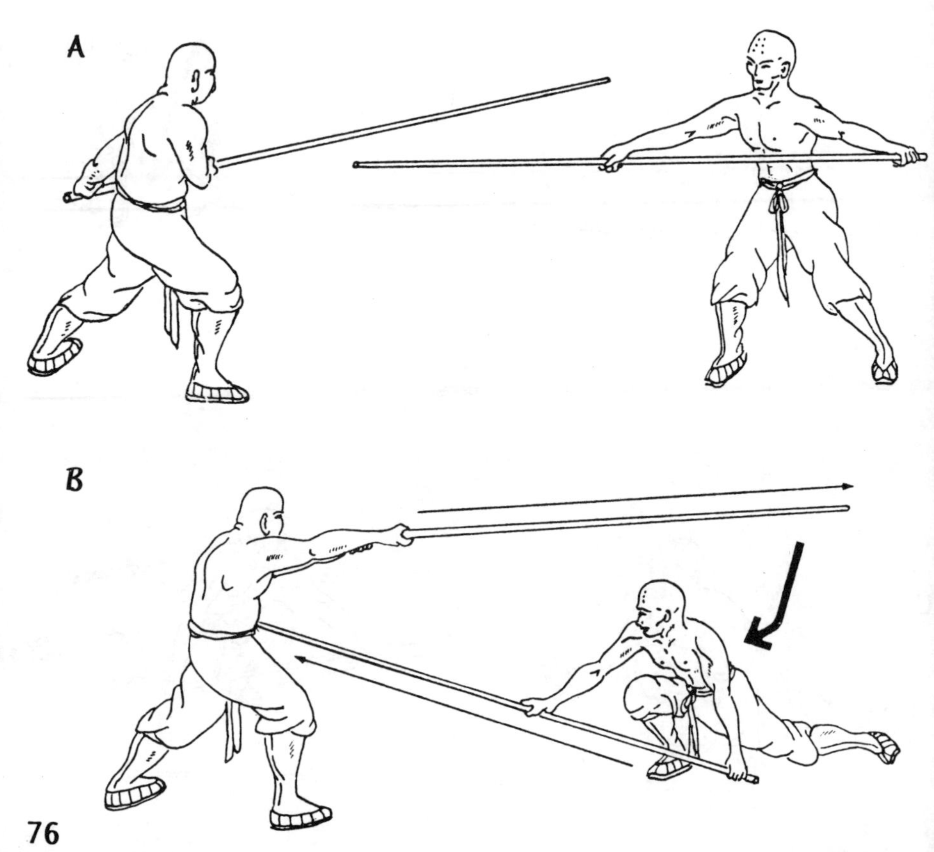

"The Backward Swing" technique to overcome "The Circling Turn" technique

The opponent launches a "Circling Turn" attack at my upper-middle level. I adopt the low kneeling stance and counter with the "Backward Swing" movement, up-lifting the end of my staff to nullify his attack and defeat him.

(My Master's comment: The most effective technique to overcome the "Circling Turn" attack is the "Backward Swing"; another technique which can also be applied for this purpose is the "Sky High Pillar")

"Look Back At The Flower" to overcome the "Kneeling on Staff" attack

I launch an attack at the opponent. He applies the "Kneeling on Staff" technique to suppress my staff. I immediately change to the "Look Back At The Flower" technique to break through his defence.

(My Master's comment: As the "Kneeling On Staff" is a very powerful technique, it is very dangerous if your enemy also applies such a technique to force you to abandon your own weapon. In case he applies this technique, just remember you should wait for no time to dissolve it before he starts or it will be too late for you do so.)

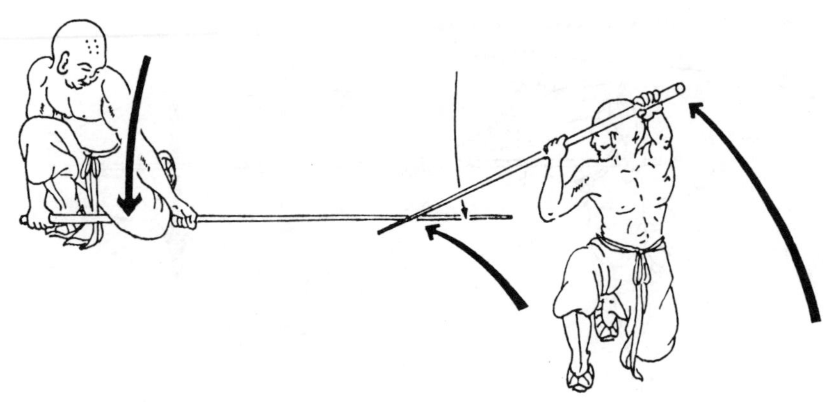

"Rock-Cracking Staff" to overcome "Look Back At The Flower" technique

I try to attack my opponent with the "Kneeling on Staff" technique, intending to suppress his staff. The opponent counters my attack with the "Look Back At The Flower" movement. At this moment I withdraw my staff and adopt the "Rock-Cracking Staff" technique to reinforce my attack.

(My Master's comment: No technique is indomitable. The "Kneeling on Staff" technique is one that is nearly impossible to defeat, except by the technique "Look Back At the Flower", which in turn can only be defeated by the "Rock-Cracking Staff" technique. It seems that regarding Kung-Fu techniques, there is a cycle in which one technique dominates another but is dominated still by another one.)

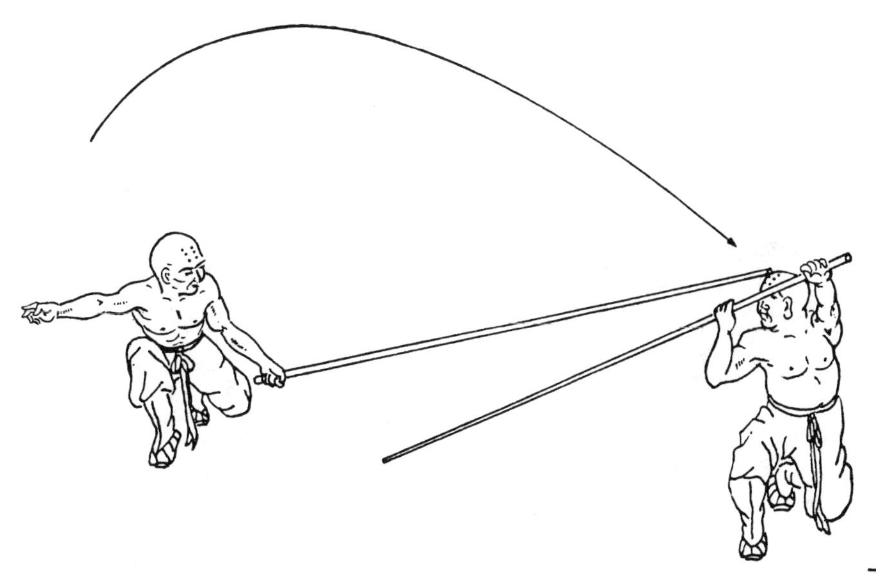

The Immortal Pointing the way" technique versus "The Downward Smash" technique; "The Upward Swing & Slant Thrust" technique versus "The Immortal Pointing The Way" technique

As I launch an attack with the "Downward Smash" technique (right in the illustration), my opponent counters with the Immortal Pointing The Way" technique. To deal with this, I adopt the "Upward Swing & Slant Thrust" technique to force my opponent to let go of his staff.

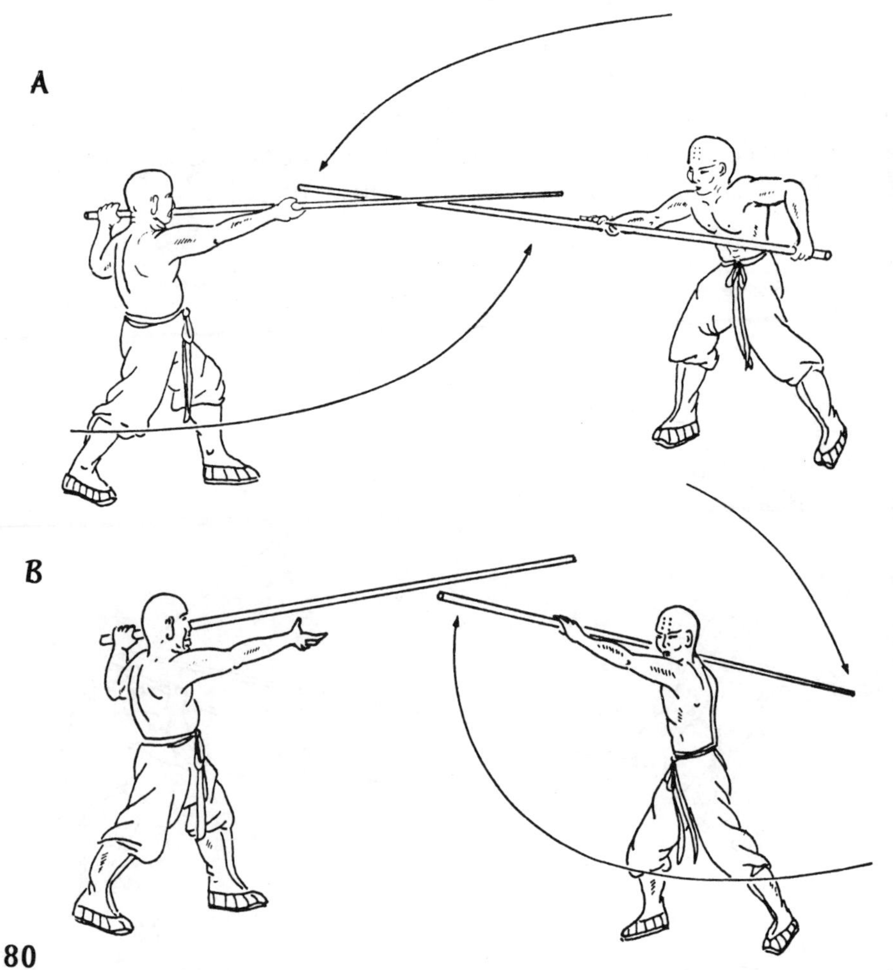

The "Horizontal Push" technique changing to the "Circle & Dart" technique

As my opponent attacks me with the "Throat Dart" technique, I nullify his attack with the "Horizontal Push" technique. After that I apply the "Circle & Dart" technique, circling my staff from below to the top of his, and then, with the "Throat Dart" technique, I thrust the end of my staff at his throat.

The "Arhat's Stretch" technique changing to the "Slant Smash & Thrust" technique

If my opponent attacks me with the "Downward Smash" technique, I can block his attack with "The Arhat's Stretch" technique. After that I turn over the end of my staff to hit the front hand of my opponent, and render a counter attack at his lower level. This is known as "The Slant Smash & Thrust" technique.

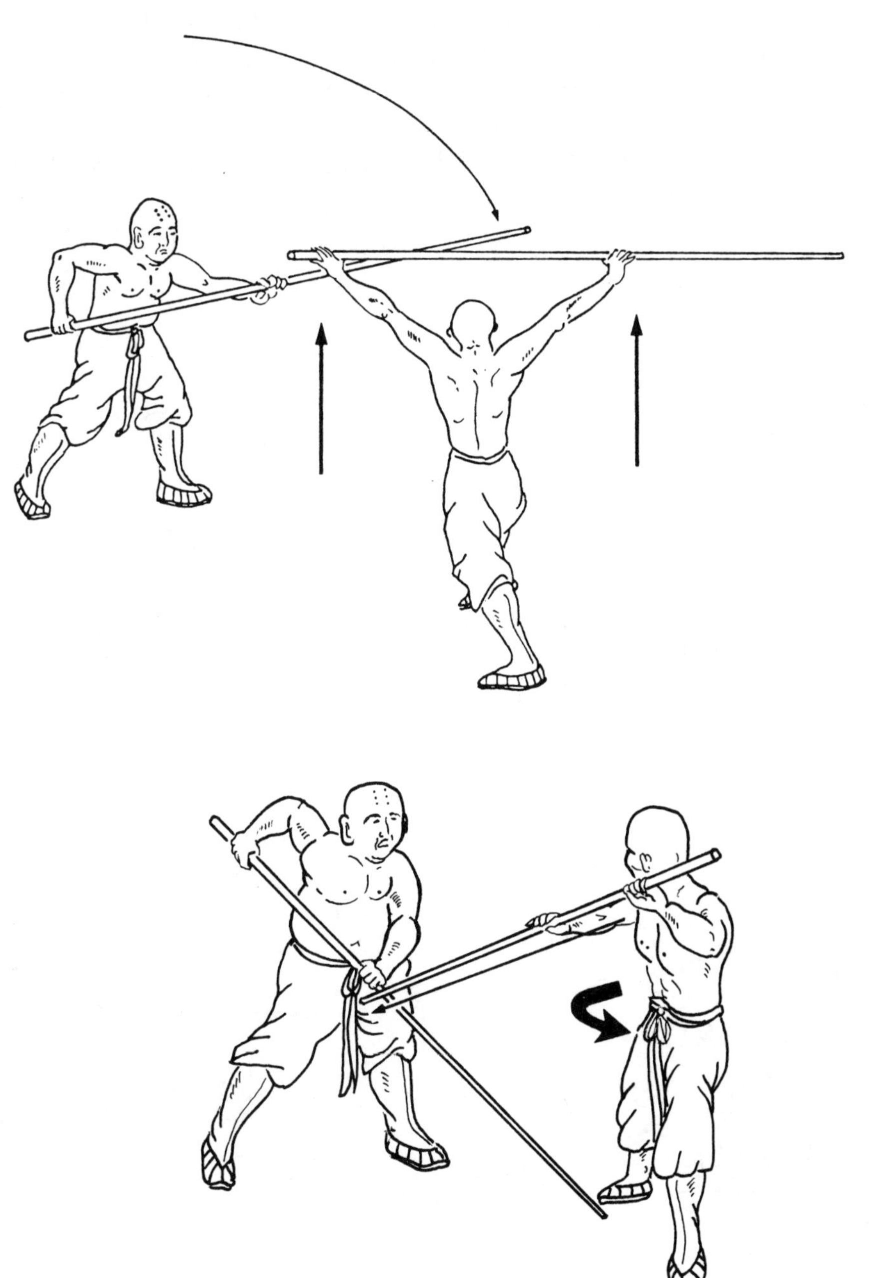

"The Dragging Spear" technique changing to "The Backward Dart" technique

If the opponent depresses my staff with his, I immediately move my left foot and pace forward while applying "The Dragging Spear" technique to nullify his attack. And before he withdraws his staff, I render a counter attack at his throat with the "Backward Dart" technique.

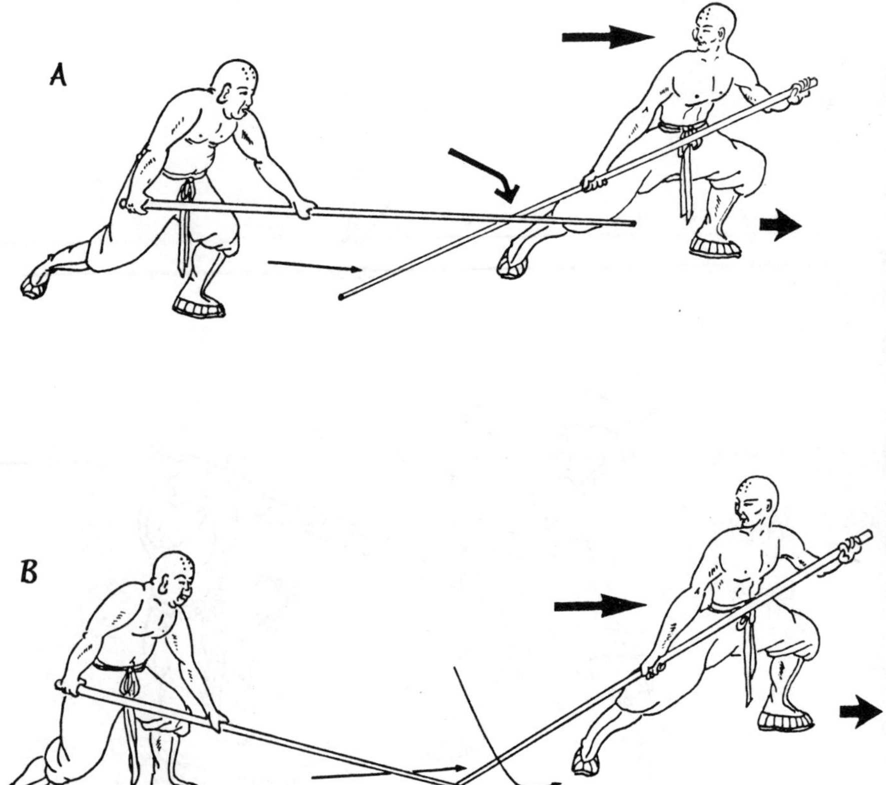

(My Master's comment:"The Dragging Spear" is a movement diverted from the famous movement known as "Emperor Kuan Dragging His Broadsword" which is believed to be a very tricky movement used by the General Kuan in the era of Three Kingdoms. This technique is applied when your enemy is using his pole or any long weapon to depress your pole or spear. You only need to step a pace away from your enemy, your weapon will be free from the pressure of your enemy's weapon. Then you have to apply the "Backward Dart" right after that.)

"The Chain Kicks"

Pretend to attack the opponent's upper level with the staff. He would set up strong defence at his upper level but neglect defence at his lower level. After that, make a surprise attack at his lower level with "Chain Kicks".

(My Master's comment: The "Chain Kicks" and the "Monkey King's Leap" are techniques better classified as kicking techniques than as staff techniques. One should not abide too much to the name of a technique, but should pay more attention to how it is applied.)

B
C

"The Monkey King's Leap" & "The Meridian Kick"

Encountering an opponent holding his staff horizontally across his chest, we can apply the technique called "The Monkey King's Leap", a swift forward leap, and then grasp the opponent's staff, and apply the Meridian Kick - a fatal kick at his groin.

(My Master's comment: The Monkey King's Leap is a technique to be followed by a surprise attacking kick such as the Meridian Kick. Psychologically, the opponent thinks you are going to attack him with your staff as you leap forward. He would thus be taken in by your under-cover kick!)

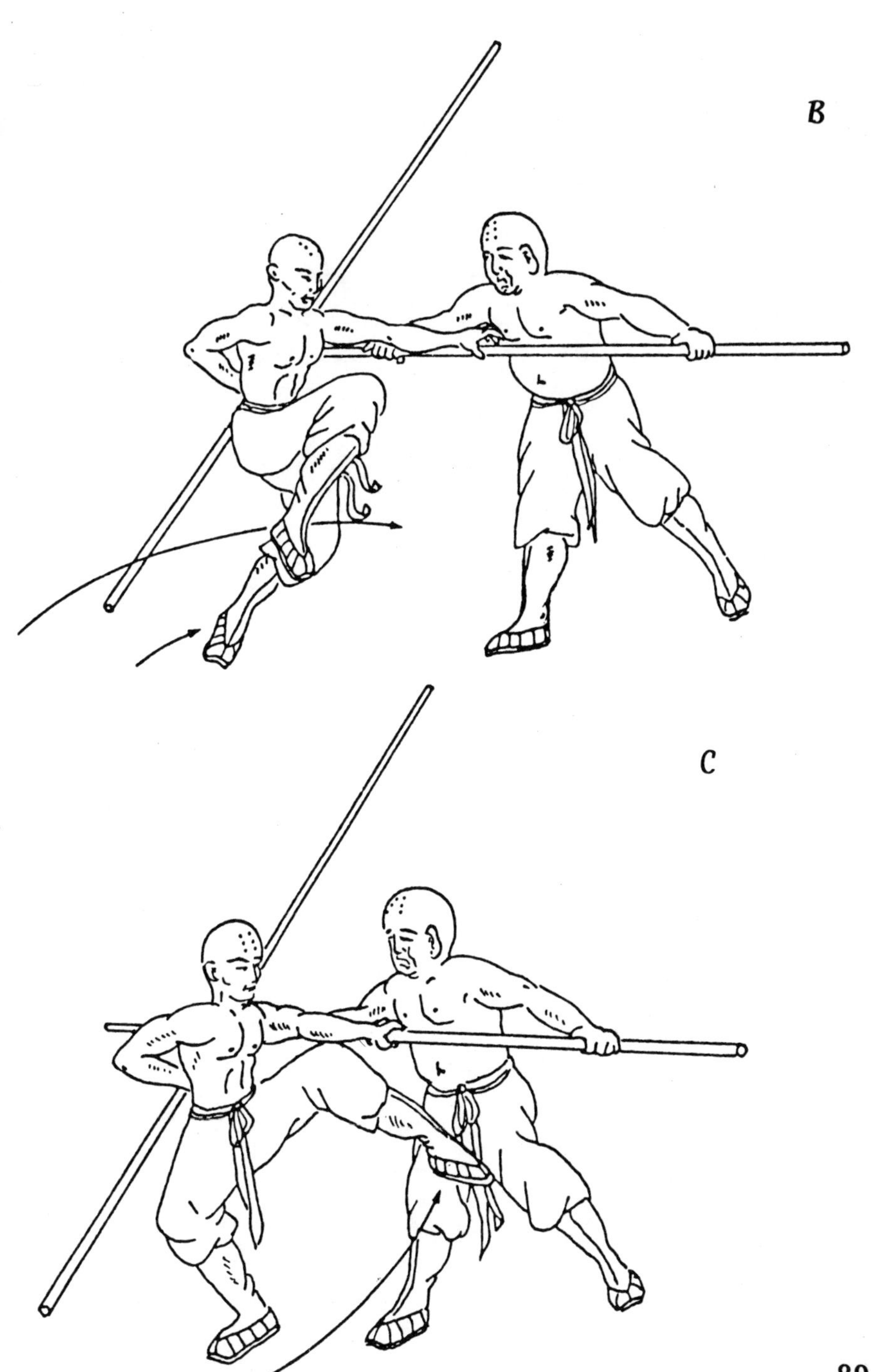
B
C

FOOTNOTES

The staff is about 7½ feet to 8½ feet in length (about 2.3 Meter to 2.6 Meter). It is commonly named by the Chinese martial artists as the **"single-headed pole"** or **"rat-tail staff"** because it is smaller at one end. This type of staff is also commonly used by wing tsun practitioners for the "**6½ Points Long Pole Techniques"** and some of the northern kungfu styles.

Belows are the addresses of the suppliers for this type of special staff (pole):——

International Wing Tsun Martial-Art Association,
U.S. Headquarters,
15227, North 23rd Place, Phoenix, AZ 85022, U.S.A.

International Wing Tsun Martial-Art Association,
European Organiozation,
SchloB, Langenzell, 6901 Wiesenbach, W. Germany.

lf-learning of the Chiese Long Weapons:—

KWAN-DAO

Backgrounds, types of long-handled broadswords, the set of Kwan-Dao, Chai-Dao vs. the bench, etc., in fully illustrated photos & descriptions, & **A BIG POSTER.**

First Time A 640 years Old Top-secret "Killer Sword Techniques" exposed!

Training system, Applications, Forms, Story, etc., now you know them all!

The Dragon-Tiger Doublesword Style

he RUNKARD KUNGFU
its applciation

ze 8½" x 5½", 162 pages.

he ONLY book on the omplete System of the Most amous Southern Style of the Eight Drunkard Immortals"!

FIVE-PATTERN HUNG KUEN *(Part I & Part II)*

You can learn *ALL* the techniques & forms of the *dragon, snake, tiger, leopard,* and *crane,* just from the illustrations & explanations.

Seven-Star Praying Mantis Kungfu

Describing ALL the fighting methods, mottos, theories, and collections of ALL the different sources, variations & developments of many branch-styles of the northern Mantis kungfu.

08 MOVEMENTS OF THE SHAOLIN OODEN-MEN HALL (Part I & Part II)

e First Time An over 100 years valuable hand-transcribed book Revealed!

SKILLS OF THE VAGABONDS

REVEALING ALL ASPECTS OF Chinese Black-Art From Where the Japanese Ninjutsu Originated!

The Ferocious-Enchanted Staff of the Ancient Monks

Original Author:	**Anonym**
Rewriter:	**Dr. Leung Ting**
Editors:	**Connie Kwong**
	Diana K.L. Yeung
Translator:	**Richard Lee**
	B.A. Hons., M.A., M.I.L.
Drawer:	**Leung Wai Choy**
Typewriter:	**Rebecca Poon**

Publisher:
Leung's Publications,

Add: 444-446 Nathan RD, 9B/Floor, Kowloon, Hong Kong.
Tel: 2388 4155 / 2775 2048 Fax: 2780 8181
E-mail: iwtahk@hkbn.net
Web site www.leungting.com / www.iwta.com

Printed in Hong Kong.

Frist Print :	October 1986
Second Print	February 1989
Third print:	June 1992
Forth Print:	January 1997
Fifth Print:	April 2002

ISBN NO. 962-7284-06-8